D1742298

MODERNIZING
SAUDI ARABIA

BY SAMAR H. FATANY

Copyright © 2013 Samar H. Fatany
All rights reserved.

ISBN: 1482509989
ISBN 13: 9781482509984

INDEX

FOREWORD

In my 10 years in Saudi Arabia, I have learned that you can count on the sun to rise and that summers will be hot and that Samar Fatany will be pushing for the societal reforms so many people believe the Kingdom must enact for the nation to progress in an ever-more competitive world.

It seems like back in 2003, many people read her pleas for social reforms with a large dose of cynical skepticism doubting that the nation would progress. Over the years, reformers have had frequent opportunities to doubt things would change, but they have changed. In this book, you will note that the road to a more modern society may still be long, but the Saudi people have traveled quite a distance up that road in a relatively short time.

A decade ago, people were talking about necessary reforms in education, industry, women in the work place, judicial reforms, more tolerance for varying points of view and economic diversification to name a few. But now there are new universities across the country, new industries and economic cities, women working in shops and offices, moves to modernize the judicial system and certainly there is more tolerance for varying points of view.

A lot of this progress can be credited to the nation's leader, King Abdullah, who seems to be determined to shepherd his flock to greener pastures and seems to have a very good idea about how to accomplish it.

I think some of that progress can be credited to the many men and women who have stood up and presented a vision of the future that certain elements of society hadn't considered and other elements of society may not have wanted to consider. The creation by the King of a national dialogue required people of varying opinions to stand up and voice their views. While it may have been easy for those representing the old establishment viewpoints, it took courage and probably some degree of risk for those who saw the ways of the modern world beyond the Kingdom's borders and realized that Saudi Arabia in some way, shape or form was a part of that world — like it or not.

Samar Fatany is one of those people who has resolutely shared her thoughts about progress, not as one with a cynical skepticism about the future but rather one who takes pride in being a Saudi and exudes the confidence that most Saudis want the best lives possible for their children, and that they realize that won't happen living in a past that no longer exists.

In this book, you'll get a little history to explain why things were like they were and why they are like they are. You'll also get an update on what's going on and where it's likely to go. One thing that is less certain may be how fast it's going to get there

I imagine it would be one of Samar Fatany's fondest wishes to write that book to let you know when you've arrived. It may be sooner than you think.

— *Stephen L. Brundage*

INTRODUCTION

This book portrays ambitious government initiatives to implement reforms and describes progressive attempts to help Saudi Arabia meet the challenges of the 21st century. It gives an overall picture of the present situation and the progress achievedso far.

It also highlights the role of women and youth as the engines for change. The book identifies women professionals in leadership roles and projects the participation of the Kingdom's youth in nation building.

The chapters outline the struggle of decision makers to deal with new realities and emphasize the process of modernizing the vast and both physically and culturally diverse regions of this country.

BRIEF HISTORY

Saudi Arabia is a huge country, 2,217,949 square kilometers, (about four times the area of France) with a wide diversity of cultures and tribes. Modernizing the society and achieving prosperity remains the greatest challenge facing reformers and the leadership in this Kingdom.

There are four main regions with widely differing local customs and traditions. The capital Riyadh is located in the central region, *Najd*, the homeland of the main Bedouin communities; the western cosmopolitan region is the *Hijaz* where the two holy cities Makkah, Medinah and the Red Sea port city of Jeddah are located;*Asir* is the rural area in the southwest quadrant of the country where the population is mainly engaged in agriculture; and finally, the Eastern region where the main oil and gas fields are located. This region has three major centers: Dhahran, the oil industry center, which is bracketed byKhobar and Dammam, the major centers for commerce. Saudi Aramco, the state-owned oil producing company is located in Dhahran. Most of the country's Shia minority livesin this region.

With the growth of the oil industry in the 1950s, the major cities increased in size due to the influx of nomadic Bedouins and villagers who left their underdeveloped remote communities to look for work. The vast demographic change was very detrimental to the development of the more urbanized areas. The nomads and villagers came in large numbers and initially worked as laborers, taxi drivers or small-scale traders. Later when they acquired further skills and education they outnumbered the local population and took over government posts, found employment in the private sector, enterednew and developing professions and went into business. They imposed their traditional Bedouin and rural customs on the once more-open, cultured cities and held a hard-line position refusing to change or modernize. The original city cultures were not recognized, and there were no policies to preserve them or grant them equal respect. As a result the tribal and rural community values became dominant.

The conservative hardliners represent the religious establishment, which shares the rule de factowith the royal family.The conservative elementwas led by descendants of Mohammad Ibn Abdul Wahab, the Al- Sheikh family who remain strong allies of the ruling family. Since the beginning of their rule the Al Saud family was bound by an agreement that gave the religious establishment control over social and religious affairs while the royal family ruled the political and economic affairs of the State. Their extreme ideology dominated the judiciary and public policy, and they continued both to have the backing of the government and to have legal authority to issue edicts and condemn anyone who did not adhere to their austere school of thought. Thus the struggle between the two cultures continues.

This struggle between the moderate reformers and the conservative hardliners reached a dangerous level when religious extremism also crept in during the seizure of the Grand Mosque in Makkah on Nov.20, 1979. Juhayman Al-Otaibi, who belonged to a powerful tribe in Najd and was a former student of the late Sheikh Abdul-Aziz Bin Baaz the grand Mufti of Saudi Arabia, led a group of Islamic dissidents calling for the return of the original ways of Islam. They attacked the Saudi rulers for spreading Western culture and demanded the expulsion of non-Muslimsfrom Saudi Arabia. Although he was arrested and beheaded along with his followers shortly after his capture, the government still enforced stricter Shariah laws and was reluctant to confront extremist elements in society. Moderate voices were denied official support, and the extremist religious scholars who controlled the courts and the education system indoctrinated the whole society with their views and a very rigid interpretation of Islam.

Then came Sept. 11, 2001, and the attack on the World Trade Center in New York, unleashing the threat of terrorism and initiating the rise of Islamophobia. As 15 of the 19 terrorist attackers ofthe 9-11 attack-swere Saudis, Saudi Arabia became a victim of terrorists and the target of a Western media campaign to demonize Saudis and Islam, based on the principle of collective guilt. Al-Qaeda terrorists and their sympathizers preyed on the minds of young Saudis and recruited them to fight against anyone who did not adhere to their militant, extremist ideology. The government reacted and started a nationwide campaign to spread awareness about this perceived threat in an attempt to protect the vulnerable and innocent Saudi young.

Meanwhile King Abdullah, then Crown Prince, initiated the Interfaith Dialogue to clarify Islam's position towards terrorism and to seek common ground between the great religions and the world's nations based on universal principles and values of peace and coexistence.

Years of national campaigns and government programs to advocate moderate Islam have passed with relentless efforts to address the threat of Islamophobia, yet extremism still exists, and Islamophobia is on the rise.

The following chapters present a glimpse into Saudi society since the attack of the Grand Mosque. Thirty three years have passed; however, extremism, cultural limitations and tribal laws rather than scholarly religious rulings of Islam continue to influence public opinion and constitute major impediments that are strangling this Kingdom and slowing the modernization process.

Chapter 1

COMBATING TERRORISM AND EXTREMISM

- Confrontation Between Tradition and Modernity
- Ijtihad a Solution to Contemporary Problems
- Positive Initiative
- Eradicating a Militant Ideology

Confrontation between Tradition and Modernity

The two Holiest cities of Islam are located in Saudi Arabia making it the center of the Muslim world. As such the Kingdom has an obligation to protect the interests of all Muslims. It is also the world's largest oil-producing country and has an international commitment to serve the interests of the global economy. The government has always given special attention to political relations with the rest of the world. However,not many Saudi citizens understand the international role of the Kingdom, and they fail to recognize the urgent need for the country to progress and be part of the 21st century global village. A nation cannot be a global leader and a medieval backwater at the same time.

The Saudi government has pushed for modernizing the Kingdom since the 1950's. However, what slowed the progress always were religious extremists who resisted any change in the traditional lifestyle.

Innovations always would be initially resisted and labeled as *Bida'ah*, meaning an un-Islamic practice, before finally being accepted by society. For example, the introduction of photography and television were met with great resistance before they were accepted and tolerated in the 1960s. Theconservative element perceives any change as a threat that could undermine their authority and control. Their ideology remains the same — intolerance toany change.

The resistance to modernization by religious scholars during the early rule of King Faisal was far greater than it is today, yet he continued to modernize the country and defied the fundamentalists without compromising Islamic values and principles.

King Faisal had several major encounters with the extremists including introducing education for women and girls, establishing the first television station, lifting the ban on music and songs and introducing pension and social insurance programs.

In 1964 King Faisal launched the first television station. This move was met with even stronger condemnation to the extent that there was an armed attack on the station. However, the encounter with the arts lasted longer. Art was never encouraged. Photography, sculpture, painting, theatre and film were prohibited. Cameras were confiscated and destroyed. It was only during King Fahd's rule in the 1970s that attempts were made to raise the cultural and artistic standards in the Kingdom.

The 1976 attack on the Grand Mosque in Makkah by extremists created a major setback for Saudi reforms and attempts to modernize the country. The militants advocated a return to medieval days and stricter religious laws, in particular an end to education for women and the abolition of television. Unfortunately, after that incident more rigid Islamic policies were imposed, and the path of progress was obstructed for many years.

The struggle to preserve archaeological sites and Saudi antiquities is another area of conflict between reformers and hard-liners and it goes on to this day. Extremists have destroyed much of the Holy Land's sacred heritage and continue to resist government initiatives to protect our valuable and historical sites in Makkahand Medinah.

During the 1990s, satellite dishes, cellular phones and the Internet were resolutely attacked before they became popular and adopted for religious affairs. Common *fatwas*, religious edicts, stated that people who watched TV, listened to music, or whose family's women did not cover their faces were sinners. Some *fatwas* even made it permissible to kill the owner of satellite TV networks because "they broadcast immoral content". It is ironic that many networks are funded and supported by Islamic programs today.

King Abdullah has taken stands against several hard-line policies and extremist scholars who were against any efforts towards change or progress. One significant example is the blatant defiance by some scholarsof the King's initiative to establish "The King Abdullah University for Science and Technology" — KAUST, a world-class research centerwith the avowed aims to serve both humanity in general and Saudi development in particular.

After the official inauguration of this coeducational research center,a senior religious official, and other extremists scholars issued a *fatwa* stating that the lack of segregation in the university was forbidden in Islam and openly condemned the move. Other extremists issued a *fatwa* stating that the lack of segregation in the university was unacceptable and un-Islamic. Fortunately the extremist scholar was later fired, and all voices against the University, the beacon of knowledge, were silenced once and for all.

King Abdullah has stated that this project stems from his desire to serve humanity and promote the true spirit of Islam. It has been his dream for many years. In his inaugural speech, the King said, "Humanity has been the target of vicious attacks from extremists who speak the language of hatred. Undoubtedly, scientific centers that embrace all peoples are the first line of defense against extremists, and today this university will become a house of wisdom to all its peers around the world, a beacon of tolerance."

Women continue to be the main target of religious extremists and the empowerment of women is still a very controversial subject within the society. The same *Ulama* (religious scholars)insist on exerting control over the lives of women and resist King Abdullah's initiatives to recognize their achievements and contributions to the nation's development.Until recently Saudi women were not allowed to appear on TV programs because of the hard-line position of the religious scholars, and their pictures were not seen in local newspapers or magazines for a very long time. They were alsonot permitted to conduct business, attend international conferences or to travel alone.

Finally with King Abdullah's rule, women began to gain more recognition. He resolutely defied the extremists'hard-line position and received accomplished women in his court encouraging them to excel and contribute. Today women activists are given the platform to influence change and call for social reform. They boldly criticize detrimental social norms on television and radio talk shows, in newspapers and magazines. Among their concerns are the issues of women driving, the guardianship rule, segregation laws, job opportunities and judicial restrictions.

Ijtihad a solution to contemporary problems

*Ijtihād,*is the Arabic word for effort. In Islamic law it is the effort to derive independent interpretations of the Quran or the sayings of the Holy Prophet, *Hadith*, and the process of creating a scholarly consensus, *Ijma* in order to address problems facing Muslims in their daily lives. During the early days of Islam, every qualified Jurist was recognized as a *Mujtahid* (a person qualified to apply his own interpretation and exercise his personal judgment in judiciary matters.) However, during the Abbasid rule, (750–1258), four legal schools of Islamic thought, *madhabs*, were established, and by the end of the 3rd century the gates of *ijtihād* were closed. Consequently all legal opinions were drawn from the established precedents, and jurists were bound to the unquestioned interpretations of the accepted four schools of thought. There were only very few scholars who attempted to contribute with their own interpretations, *Ijtihad* such as Ibn Taymīah (1236–1328) and Jalāl ad-Dīn as-Suyūtī (1445–1505).

It was not until the 19th and 20th centuries that Muslim scholars revived *Ijtihad* in order to adapt to scientific advancements, technological developments and modern lifestyles of a modern world."

The emergence of Muslim leaders and scholars who boldly have asserted the need to adapt to new realities is indeed a major development that can energize the process of *ijtihad*— the interpretation of Islamic law — and help Muslims find solutions to contemporary problems.

Addressing the 36th annual meeting of the Islamic Development Bank in June 2011, Minister of Finance Ibrahim Al-Assaf urged Muslim countries to adapt to the changing global environment in order to confront the challenges facing the Muslim world today.

Many Muslim scholars, Arab and non-Arab, have stressed the need to revive the process of *ijtihad*, or the interpretation of Islamic law and recognize it as an Islamic science to enable Muslims of the 21st century to preserve their faith and apply the true tenets of Islam to their present-day needs.

To confront the new challenges and energize the process of *ijtihad*, however, Muslim countries need to conduct Shariah studies, encourage moderate and competent scholars, reform the educational system and upgrade Muslim academic councils. Only then can a more educated interpretation be adopted to serve the needs of the contemporary Muslim society effectively.

It is unfortunate that religious scholars terminated the practice of *ijtihad* 500 years ago and adopted a more conservative and negative stance toward innovation and adaptation. When the door of *ijtihad* was closed, a consensus was established that there would be no more independent reasoning in religious law and that all Muslims should follow the interpretation of the doctrine by the scholars of that era once and for all.

Today we live in a very different world from that of half a millennium ago, and Muslims need to find solutions to contemporary problems that did not exist in the past. Moderate religious scholars today assert that *ijtihad* should remain an essential part of the Muslim tradition even if others disagree. The rigid interpretations of Islamic law by hardliners no longer provide suitable solutions to the challenges facing the Muslim world of today.

Conservative Muslims insist on keeping the doors to *ijtihad* closed. They argue that most Muslims today do not have the training in legal sources to conduct *ijtihad*. The moderates, however, assert that any competent scholar can perform *ijtihad* given that Islam has no generally accepted clerical hierarchy.

Conservative scholars need to be reminded that Shariah law is based on two basic principles. They are: what is in essence beneficial is permitted (*halal*) and what is in essence harmful is prohibited (*haram*). Shariah law is based on the principle that always adopts the easier alternative after comparing a few of the available relevant cases; therefore, the general rule for interpretation includes the removal of the rigid or the doubtful and applying a balance between the two.

It is time to eliminate the weak sayings of the Prophet, *Hadith*, and derive rulings only from the authentic ones. We cannot continue to allow only one legal authority on the interpretation of Shariah laws or recognize only one absolute judgment on judicial issues. Moderate scholars maintain that there could be more than one answer resulting from *ijtihad* on a particular issue — each ruling depending on the circumstances surrounding the situation.

During the 8th and 9th centuries, the progressive religious scholars who were keen to understand and apply Islamic rulings to changing realities developed the system of *ijtihad*. Unfortunately, after that there were few capable scholars who were willing to address old laws that did not apply to new social, economic and scientific developments. Today, however, we are finally witnessing concerted efforts to revive *ijtihad* and address some of the challenges of the 21st century.

For example, the economic and social reality of contemporary life has created many complicated problems for Muslims living in the United States. They had financial and social difficulties and needed direction from a Muslim religious authority. Ultimately the Councils of Muslim Scholars in Europe and the United States decreed that it was permissible for Muslims residing in the West to buy houses with mortgages and to pay interest on these loans. Although this was contrary to Shariah law that forbids charging and paying interest, the Muslim scholars gave their consent declaring that it was a necessary rule for Muslims to meet their financial and social needs in the West. Meanwhile, Muslim countries are working hard to train more Shariah experts who are needed to define Shariah-compliant rules and support Islamic finance.

Other modern problems that needed attention include test-tube babies, organ donations, cloning and various current issues in science that require an Islamic ruling. It goes without saying that we need pious scholars with a wider scope of knowledge who are experts in Arabic linguistics, social and political sciences, economics, international and Shariah laws to be delegated to exercise *ijtihad*.

Muslims should also be wary of people with limited education who have reopened the doors to *ijtihad* and have taken a more rigid direction. In order to revive the process global Muslim organizations need to support global initiatives to train more scholars in methods of deduction so as to draw more accurate and logical conclusions. There is also a need to establish a stricter code to identify or accept a *Hadith* as authentic. It is crucial for Muslims today to encourage Islamic researchers who can conduct studies on the aims and purposes of the Shariah law. No one should be allowed to give a ruling without an understanding of the events surrounding a Qura'nic revelation or derive laws in matters with no explicit judgment in the texts, or matters which cannot be defined or explained.

Fundamentalists who have confused and misguided many innocent believers have hijacked the principles of Islam. Moderates today reject past controversial conditions that were dictated by earlier scholars and continue to be a source of public disagreement. Muslim countries need to support a global consensus to restore the science of *ijtihad* among Islamic sciences and eliminate extremist practices not relevant to modern times. They must exert greater efforts to adapt to the changing global economic, social and scientific environment.

Reforming the curriculum of Islamic studies is also important. Unfortunately students were not exposed to the four schools of thought. Religious scholars in the past would say, "This is my opinion, and I could be wrong. And this is someone else's opinion, and he could be right." Fundamentalists have yet to understand that no one has absolute authority on the truth.

There are currently several national and international councils of jurisprudence and interpretations of Shariah; however, to be effective they need to upgrade the qualifications of their members.

There have been recent attempts by Islamic councils of jurisprudence to work together collaboratively in order to be more effective and to serve the interests of the Muslim world. There are also increasing demands from Muslim countries to include Women and professionals from all walks of life in religious councils. Such councils must rise to the expectations of Muslims and make wise judgments and formulate legislation on pressing issues of our time, such as the status of women, Muslim lifestyles, Islamic economies, the situation of Muslims in non-Muslim societies, the relation between the Muslims and the West and so on.

An efficient and strong judiciary is a fundamental requirement for the protection of human rights and for sustainable economic progress and development. Let us hope that the higher judicial institute at Imam Mohammed University contributes towards the development of a uniform justice system in Saudi Arabia and removesthe culturally biased attitudes that are resistant to progressive thinking and encourages a more efficient Saudi judiciary. The graduates of the institute hold a critical responsibility to serve the needs of the 21st century Saudi citizen.

Eradicating a Militant Ideology

The concept of *Takfir* or excommunication for Muslims is the equivalent of apostasy. The notion of *takfir* has been used by militant and terrorist organizations to justify the killing of innocent people, Muslims as well as non-Muslims.

A major anti-*takfir* campaign was organized nationwide to confront the influence of the deviant militant ideology that is threatening the Muslim world today. The initiative aims to tackle religious extremism and eradicate the *takfiri* militant ideology that has crept into the peaceful and spiritual Saudi society.

This militancy is one of the greatest challenges that this nation faces today. In order to address this threat, the government has begun a large-scale campaign nationwide to promote moderation and tolerance among Saudi citizens.

The government has begun in earnest a campaign to address the issue of *takfir*, the labeling of a Muslim as an infidel or unbeliever, which is one of the principal reasons behind the intolerance and strife that is prevalent among many in our society today. Unfortunately, this concept has been allowed to spread unchecked for too long, and as a result we are now faced with a generation that has been misguided by a deviant ideology. We are compelled to tackle this dangerous ideology head-on as they have taken the liberty of distorting the Qur'an and *Hadith*.

The Saudi Government has recognized that there is a desperate need for an effective awareness campaign to inform the public about the dangers of extremism and to protect the young from the instigators of instability within the society. Saudi citizens nationwide should all support the Ministry of Interior in its goal of eliminating this threat. The few brave and moderate religious scholars should be commended for speaking out against the proponents of the *takfiri* concept.

One of the most significant initiatives of the Ministry of Interior was the inauguration of an international conference on *takfir* in 2011. In cooperation with Imam Mohammed bin Saud Islamic University, the "Prince Naif bin Abdul Aziz International Prize for the Prophet's Sunnah and Contemporary Islamic Studies" organized a three-day conference to address the impact of *takfir* on the future of Islam. More than 100 researchers from 45 countries were invited to participate. The key objective was to highlight the responsibility of social institutions in addressing the threat as well as draw up strategies to curb the spread of the extremist ideology. The conference was held in the holy city of Medinah, and it coincided with lectures and workshops held nationwide. The participants discussed ways to tackle the concept of *takfir* and raise awareness about the distorted views that produced a negative impact on Saudi citizens in particular.

The conference was the first of many other initiatives that have been organized to curb the spread and influence of extremists on the young. The ultimate goal is to protect Saudi society from the deviant ideology that promotes violence and hostility between people. There are *takfiris* who believe that any Muslim who commits a sin, whether major or minor, is an infidel, *kafir*,but there are others who believe that it has to be a major sin. However, the more dangerous extremists label any Muslim who does not share their extreme religious views as *kafir*. They go as far as making his lifea legitimate target to attack or kill.

The three-day conference was an opportunity to allow Muslim scholars to address the threat and come up with recommendations to curb the spread of this dangerous phenomenon and negate its anti-Islamic views.

The distorted interpretation of the concept of *takfir* in Islam has misguided many of the young who remain behind bars for committing terrorist acts and have become a danger to themselves and society. Religious extremists used this concept to recruit many young people, legitimizing their actions in the name of Islam. It is truly unfortunate that the perpetrators of this ideology have succeeded in manipulating the minds of innocent youths and they subsequently masterminded terrorist operations that continue to threaten the Muslim world at large.

The attempt on the life of Deputy Interior Minister Prince Muhammad bin Naif in 2010 by a 22-year-old suicide bomber shocked and alarmed the public and exposed the evil and vicious deviant ideology that continues to prey on the minds of the young and uses them to carry out criminal acts to further their own political agendas while defiling Islam. The terrorists and their sympathizers have been very active while many imams, parents and government agencies have failed to recognize the extent of the threat to this peaceful society.

The Saudi government campaign to address this dangerous phenomenon needs to be supported and encouraged by the whole society as well as Muslim scholars all over the world. The *takfiri* ideology today threatens to create conflict both within and between all Muslim communities. This phenomenon needs to be eradicated before it causes more chaos and instability within the Muslim world at large. Those who adhere to the extremist *takfiri* ideology have disassociated themselves from their societies and have chosen to be in constant confrontation with their fellow Muslims who reject their extremist views and principles.

Meanwhile, another major conference to address violence and extremism was held at Umm Al-Qura University in the holy city of Makkah on Sept 19, 2011. The fourth Teachers' Preparation Conference was held on the theme, "Teachers' responsibility toward the phenomenon of violence and extremism in the light of changes of the present age and the requirements of citizenship." Senior education officials and specialists gathered for three days to study the effects of teachers' values and attitudes on students.

Researchers held that teachers with hard-line views played a vital role in misguiding the youth and allowing them to be easily recruited by militants and terrorist organizations. The government has allocated millions to upgrade the education system and to prepare programs to enhance teachers' performance. Unqualified educators have been up to neither the expectations of the state nor society. Nurturing and guiding the young is the national and religious responsibility for all members of society — especially the teaching faculty.

The unrest and turmoil in Saudi Arabia's neighboring countries and the negative influence of extremists who deviously manipulate the innocent minds of our youth continues to be of serious concern to the state. It is a responsibility of both the state and academic institutions to inform and educate the public about the danger that lies within and to offer a peaceful and healthy environment for all citizens of this land. The role of educators cannot be stressed enough in this process. Education can protect the youth from all elements with selfish agendas who threaten our harmony and peaceful way of life. The government has initiated an extensive training program to upgrade the skills of educators, raise their level of awareness and instill in them the Muslim values of moderation and tolerance, which are the firmament of universal peace and prosperity.

Gradually the nationwide campaign to combat extremism and foster tolerance and understanding among one another is gaining momentum. Many citizens hope that this development will help ease the tensions and conflicts in the daily lives of people and allow them to enjoy a harmonious society by showing respect for others who may not share their own views. This awareness campaign is a vital step that should allow everyone to recognize the social ills that have led to extremism and created such a hostile environment. The fight against discrimination has begun. What is needed now is to support a more humane and moderate attitude, so that Muslims can live with the true principles of their faith.

Chapter 2

THE REFORM MOVEMENT

- King Abdullah Initiates Reforms
- Reforming the Judiciary
- Action against Corruption
- Economic and SocialReforms
- Educational Reforms

King Abdullah Initiates Reform

The reform movement is an ambitious initiative that involves vision, wisdom, strength and perseverance to pave the way towards a prosperous 21st century state.

Modernizing Saudi Arabia is not an easy task. There are major challenges to overcome and enormous work to be done. The King has become a symbol of strength and reassurance to his citizens since his ascension to the throne. His support and encouragement, particularly to women and the young, has endeared him as a father figure and as a king to be respected and revered.

The most significant reforms addressed sixmajor challenges that stood in the way of modernizing Saudi Arabia, specifically: combating terrorism, confronting extremism and the hard-line position against women, reforming the judiciary, implementing social and economic reforms and upgrading the educational system.

Upon his ascension to the throne King Abdullah initiated political reforms to confront the danger of terrorism and the deviant ideology that was threatening the security and stability of Saudi Arabia.. He initiated an aggressive national rehabilitation program to combat terrorism, and encouraged a major campaign to propagate moderation and fight extremism. He supported the global war on terror and was also able to save the country from a plot to brand it as a terrorist state to be targeted and attacked. He succeeded in defusing an international media campaign that seemed to implicate Saudi Arabia in terrorism and distort the image of its people the world over. King Abdullah wisely led a counter offensive by reaching out to all leaders around the world calling for peace and global prosperity. Many international journalists were invited to access firsthand information about the culture and the peaceful nature of the Saudi people. The monarch welcomed foreign investments to contribute to the country's development plans, and he initiated the intercultural dialogue to bridge the divide between Islam and the West.

In August 2010, King Abdullah decreed that only officially approved religious scholars would be allowed to issue *fatwas*, putting a stop to many spurious *fatwas* that did not represent the true spirit of Islam. King Abdullah boldly defied the extremists' hard-line position that marginalized women, and he received accomplished women in his court, encouraging them to excel and contribute.

The government has also taken major steps to enforce regulations that support the role of women in society. In 2006, identification cards for women became mandatory, despite the uproar by the *Ulema*(religious scholars) who were against the inclusion of a woman's photo on the card and remain dissatisfied with the directive to this day. Accordingly the ID card was required for all government and business transactions.

In 2008, after continued demands and pressure from the professional and business community, a ban on single woman renting hotel rooms was lifted, and women could travel freely within the Kingdom. In 2011 the ban on women working in lingerie stores was finally lifted creating jobs for women across the Kingdom.

In 2011, the King openly defied the hardliners in his speech to the Shoura Council criticizing their hard-line positions and granting women political rights. His strong statement reassured the people that progress will continue, and Saudi Arabia will continue to modernize and reform.

He announced that women would be allowed to vote and run in municipal elections in 2015, and they will become members of the next session of the Shoura Council in 2012. In his inaugural speech to the Shoura Councilafter he took the throne he strongly rejected any marginalization of women and welcomed their participation in the decision-making process.

Reforming the Judiciary

Reforming the judiciary is one of the major challenges facing the Kingdom. A Royal Decree was issued in 2007 to reform the judiciary system and improve human rights in Saudi Arabia. A budget of 7 billion riyals has been allocated to upgrade the judiciary, a new supreme court as well as regional appeals courts, specialized courts and family courts were established to provide better services and more rapidly delivered rulings in many cases. The Ministry of Justice also increased the number of judges by 150 across the court system in an effort to expedite court proceedings and dispose of cases as soon as possible.

However, the implementation of reforms has been very slow. The slow judicial reforms make it difficult to put an end to corruption and human rights violations that jeopardize the due process of law. An ineffective judiciary both denies citizens the settlement of disputes and creates grievances by unjust treatment and mediation. Saudi courts need to uphold the rule of law to ensure justice for all.

The new judiciary law has not been fully implemented because hardliners still have influence on the legal system, and they continue to adhere to rigid interpretations of Shariah laws denying justice to many citizens in this country. Only judges from the Hanbali school of thought are appointed, while the more moderate scholars and judges of the *Hejaz* region, who adhere to other more moderate schools of thought, are marginalized. Different judges issue varying rulings according to each one's interpretation of Shariah law.

One of the most significant developments of 2011 was the decision to allow only the senior members of the *Ulama* to issue religious edicts (*fatwas*). This rule put a stop to the embarrassing *fatwas*, which were illogical and irrelevant and not based on any authentic hadith or Qura'nic verse, that were broadcast on satellite channels.

There have been frequent calls to codify Shariah laws, but Sharia scholars have been reluctant to consider the move. Various jurisprudence academies have been studying the matter for the past several decades, and the matter is still pending.

According to Dr. Abdul Rahman Al Sanad, a professor at the Department of Comparative Jurisprudence at the Higher Institute of Judiciary, the council of senior religious scholars has finally submitted a project to codify and document the verdicts issued by the Kingdom's Sharia courts for the consideration of higher authorities. He said the documentation would help judges avoid making inconsistent judgments on identical cases, and it would also allow people to know in advance what they can expect in any dispute on the basis of precedent. However most of the verdicts issued in Saudi courts have been based on a rigid interpretation of Islam; therefore, the moderates and people who adhere to different schools of thought would not accept them.

The more positive side of the project are the studies conducted on the developments in international laws and comparing those laws with Shariah laws with due consideration to social, psychological, security and economic global factors.

During a seminar titled, "Human Rights in the New Legal System," two judges from the general court in Jeddah, Hamid Al-Arwan and Abdullah Al-Arwan, stressed the importance of spreading the culture of human rights in legal circles. They noted that there is a need to codify laws to make the legal system easier for the public to understand.

They explained that most of the laws and regulations in the Arab World are based on the jurisprudence of various Islamic schools of thought. Since 1870, however, some Muslim countries supported the codification, and others opposed it. Today the implementation of Sharia codes depends on the decision of the rulers.

Meanwhile, the training programs funded by the Ministry of Justice have had little success in improving the performance of all its employees. Saudi lawyers are seeking protection from vindictive judges who issue rulings to penalize them. There are instances in which some judges have ordered lawyers to be imprisoned for 24 hours due to minor disagreements. Waleed Shaira a legal consultant in Riyadh has commented, "Lawyers should be immune from judges or investigation officials who punish them due to courtroom disagreements. There should be a special council to decide whether a lawyer should be penalized or not."

Legal consultant and member of the national committee for lawyers, Mohammad Al-Mushawwah, noted, "Some judges and commission officials violate the rights of lawyers and behave arbitrarily due to the absence of specific regulations against such hard-line practices."

Positive Initiatives

The Judiciary continues to suffer due to a lack of qualified judges and legal experts. The plan to establish a Higher Institute for Judicial Studies at Imam Muhammad Islamic University in Riyadh is a step in the right direction. It is among the major initiatives to support the reforms in the Saudi judicial system. Master- and doctoral-degree programs will be introduced to create skilled graduates qualified to better serve justice. The training that will be provided at the Higher Institute is expected to produce more uniformity and professionalism in the present judicial system.

Dr.Suleiman AbalKhayl, rector of the university has said that, "The institute will facilitate the supervision of candidates for the judicial service; the institute will gather the largest number of legal experts. so that the trainees and students can get quality training about the Kingdom's legal system, and the institute will also conduct workshops, seminars and training sessions for judges, assistant judges and notaries."

The institute will have a major role in producing legal experts with specialized qualifications to address complex jurisprudence. A judge's knowledge and expertise is the foundation of fair and just rulings. More competent and efficient judges can expedite the delayed court procedures that are prolonging the misery of many innocent victims. Justice delayed is justice denied.

The Ministry of Justice has announced an Advisory Council comprised of representatives of the General Presidency of the Scholarly Research and *Ifta*, the Supreme Judiciary Council, the Supreme Court, the Ministry of Justice, the Court of Grievances and the Prosecution and Investigations Commission will be established to coordinate between the institute and the bodies that are represented on the council. The advisory council has a responsibility to promote a more understanding judiciary that recognizes and accepts all schools of Islamic thought and addresses controversial matters in order to provide justice.

The institute will also ensure that judicial courts implement the recommended methods. The specialized courts that have been established to avoid conflict over jurisprudence need experts who are more familiar with contemporary legal issues in labor and commercial disputes, as well as civil and criminal cases.

The Saudi judiciary must be more familiar with international law and should recognize that the existing rigid interpretation of Sharia law needs to be revised to better serve the needs of Saudi society. Saudis today can no longer live in the past and remain isolated from the rest of the world. Hardliners must be made to understand that we live in a global village that is very competitive and interconnected.

The establishment of the Islamic Jurisprudence Complex in Saudi Arabia is yet another promising development. It is vital today to address seriously and agree on the Shariah perspectives on contemporary affairs to create a more cohesive Muslim nation that respects all sects. Muslims must seek a common ground that unites them and avoid matters of divergence.

Currently there are many young Shariah graduates well aware of the need to implement new laws and regulations that can address the needs of all citizens and residents. Lawyers United is a team of talented young law graduates who are keen to use their knowledge and research to call for the enactment of laws and regulations that guarantee the rights of all Saudi citizens. The team recently debated the negative consequences of multiple marriages. They called for a law that would enforce the Sharia conditions for multiple marriages. They argued that judges should not approve multiple marriages without official documents that prove the financial and social ability of the groom to support more than one wife.

The Sharia graduates asserted that according to Saudi social scientists, Saudi families are suffering due to the negligence of fathers who are reckless and irresponsible. They marry more than one wife without respecting the conditions dictated by God to provide equal financial support, care and attention to each. They demanded legal intervention to stop the disintegration of Saudi families and the negative consequences of multiple marriages that include unhappy children, miserable mothers, juvenile delinquents, drug addicts and unproductive citizens.

The Ministry of Justice has lately provided some hope for employing Saudi woman lawyers who continue to call for their right to practice their profession and an opportunity to defend women's rights. The Ministry has promised to appoint women as legal experts in the courts of grievances across several provinces. Positions include researchers in judiciary, researchers in Sharia, legal researchers and administrative assistants. There are also plans to employ women law graduates in the Investigations Department.

This is a positive development that could serve many abused women who suffer as a result of the long legal proceedings. Female legal representatives can now expedite proceedings and can offer counseling and assistance to women waiting to appear in court. More than 70percent of those who come to courts are women. Allowing women lawyers to assist them would certainly help many women who are in a desperate need of a woman attorney to confide in and with whom to be more at ease when discussing their personal affairs.

These developments may seem impressive; however, many critics have begun to lose faith and criticized the halfhearted approach to tackle the challenges blocking the implementation of judicial reforms

The ministries of Justice and Social Affairs have welcomed recommendations by Saudi researchers to address social injustice and severe court rulings. One example is the accepted study conducted by a judge in RasTanura that concluded jail terms and lashings were overused and failed, only contributing to a high rate of recidivism. The study recommended alternative sentences including community service, such as cleaning mosques, planting trees and helping at care homes for the elderly. Such recommendations are often implemented in more advanced societies and have contributed in reforming and rehabilitating juveniles. We should employ them here.

A vigorous national campaign has been launched to defend the rights of children and put a stop to child-abuse cases that were left unchecked for too long. Community doctors and social workers continue to call for more stringent laws to combat the rise in domestic violence and to penalize parents who fail to provide proper care for their children.

Action against corruption

In 2011, King Abdullah ordered the prompt formation of the Anti Corruption Commission after devastating floods hit Jeddah. The floods exposed not only the weakness of the physical infrastructure, but also the corruption of government officials and the negligence of civil servants who were because of it, responsible for the destruction of whole districts in the city, killing hundreds and ruining the lives of thousands of innocent people. The tragedy paved the way for more serious government measures to end corruption and bureaucracy, illegal land grabs, the embezzlement of government funds and the abuse of power for personal gain.

The investigation that followed was an indication that the government was serious about fighting corruption and more determined to implement reforms.

A number of relevant bylaws have been issued to crack down on bribery and corrupt practices in the workplace and in government. The King has warned that no one is immune; therefore ,ministers if convicted of involvement in corruption could be removed from their positions and imprisoned.

Lately there have been attempts focusing more on court administration and capacity building with less attention to problems related to judicial independence and accountability. Much money has been spent automating the courts to reduce workloads and to modernize case management. Universally, however, legal experts warn that when these reforms are not accompanied by increased accountability, it increases the risk of making corrupt courts more efficiently corrupt.

Members of Saudi society need to show more respect for the law and implement work ethics to accelerate reforms. Reformers and legislators both must act with a greater sense of responsibility and a commitment to stop corruption and serve public interests.

Economic and social reforms

The World Bank recognized Saudi Arabia as one of the top ten reformers in the world. High oil prices and heavy government spending boosted the national economy, initiating large scale development plans across the country that included the underdeveloped regions, which had been neglected for a long time.

The government stepped up its economic reforms in 2012 and allocated a SR400 billion budget on infrastructure projects across all governorates and rural centers as well as enhancing public services for all citizens and residents.

Extensive studies were conducted to improve public services. SomeSR130 billion was introduced to support housing-development plans; loans up to SR10.67 billion were provided for the construction of 500 thousand houses.

Projects were initiated to address major challenges of unemployment, the diversification of the economy, reducing reliance on state-run industries and spending on welfare.

Financial, legal and labor reforms were introduced to provide transparency in laws and regulations to facilitate trade and foreign investments needed to expedite and develop infrastructure projects.

Legal changes were put in place to improve the enforcement of contracts and help smaller enterprises obtain loans and ease the risks to make lending less restrictive.

Dr.Abdul Aziz Aldakheel, a prominent financial analyst, disclosed at a recent real estate forum that economic reforms addressed the needs of the low-income groups, which included 82 percent of Saudis. He said this was a group most in need of housing, and the government should assume responsibility. Bank officials in charge of marketing loans say that a large number of citizens took loans that they then struggled to repay. Most of them take loans to spend on holidays or on weddings or expensive cars; others take loans to build or renovate. Social researchers say that Saudi families are now entangled in debts and are unable to pay them off. Most of them do not know how to plan financially.

The reforms included a SR1billion riyal increase in the social security budget, a 15 percent increase in aid for unemployed young people plus payment of their tuition fees.

The private-sector growth, entrepreneurship, employment and education were also high on the agenda of economic reforms.

Addressing the vast dependency on foreign labor, the government initiated the, "The Second Phase of Saudization" process of the private sector designed to increase the number of Saudi employees in private firms and tackle the rising unemployment problem, which had reached 35 percent according to unofficial estimates. Most job seekers were between the ages of 20 and 24.

The first phase was ineffective mainly because Saudi graduates neither had the qualifications nor the skills needed in the market due to the pooreducation standards. Moreover, the labor market was saturated with graduates in social sciences and religious studies, literature and history. The workforce needed graduates in technical, engineering, scientific and medical programs, business administration and computer science. Creating better skilled and employable graduates required reforming the education system, restructuring the labor market and building capacity.

The main focus was on creating economic opportunities to support social welfare and provide education and training to develop the skills required by the job market. The government imposed minimum quotas of Saudi employees on companies and decreed that only Saudis staff certain businesses such as gold retailers, car dealerships and travel agencies. More emphasis was placed on education, vocational training and on-the-job training.

In a serious effort to address unemployment the *Nitaqat* government project was launched to create new job opportunities for Saudis. The scheme grades businesses into various ranks according to the percentage of Saudis they employ; the greater the percentage, the better the grading. The government program penalizes companies that fail to reach minimum quota of Saudis in their workforce, and they are rewarded if they greatly exceed the target.

According to M. Mosley a former investment broker who managed the government scheme, the government was working in cooperation with the private sector to make school graduates more employable. Some of these initiatives included, job fairs, job subsidies and regulations intended to push the private sector into hiring more Saudi citizens instead of foreigners.

King Abdullah initiated the *Hafiz* program to pay a monthly stipend of 2,000 riyals a month for unemployed Saudis for up to a year until they can find employment in government or private sectors. The Ministry of Labor also sponsored career exhibitions in cities across the Kingdom to

assess the potentials of job seekers and refer them to pos   sr
More than 80percent of the beneficiaries were women.

The program was ambitious and could have had a grea
of the job seekers were still unemployable ,however, and did not have une
proper skills or adequate knowledge to qualify them for any of the available
jobs. Many needed social rehabilitation and vocational skills while others
needed to understand discipline and work ethics, and a large group needed
proper training and better educational standards.

The economic challenges facing Saudi society are overwhelming, and
we have a long way to go to achieve the desired goals.

Educational Reforms

Major Strides Towards Educational Excellence

Every national day we celebrate our achievements and review our prospects
for a more prosperous future. With each year of reforms we have every
reason to celebrate accomplishments achieved in many fields ,particularly
in the educational system that has been at the forefront of all reforms. The
government so far has implemented various educational reforms to meet
the challenges of the modern world.

King Abdullah's reformist ideas addressed the extremists control over
the curriculum that was being taught in schools spreading intolerance
toward other cultures and religions. Schools were monitored to curb the
development of extremist ideas. The Ministry of Education changed the
Islamic studies curriculum to include more moderate interpretations of the
Qur'an with greater emphasis on research and sciences. Elementary and
middle school curricula were revised to include more English, science, history and social studies. Mathematics and science classes were improved.
The government has recognized three major projects to raise the quality of education, mainly to develop creativity and excellence among faculty members, establishing centers for research and scientific excellence
and promoting a scientific research culture among students in order to
raise the quality of higher education. Training programs were provided
for teachers to implement innovative methods in teaching and learning,
and new techniques in the classrooms support critical thinking and inspire

dents to be creative and alert. Mentoring programs were also introduced to build character and confidence, help students discover their capabilities and potentials and keep up-to-date with global trends and developments. However, implementation of these ambitious projects has been poor, and upgrading the educational system remains our greatest challenge.

In 2012 King Abdullah launched an SR81.5 billion budget to boost higher education programs across all regions of the Kingdom. New universities were established in each region and a university branch in each governorate in order to provide all citizens educational opportunities. Large sums were allocated for scientific research and the establishment of technology incubators. King Abdullah University of Science and Technology offered doctoral degrees in chemical and biological engineering, applied mathematics, environmental, chemical and computer science.

The Ministry of Education addressed many challenges to upgrade the quality of education in the Kingdom. To begin with the Ministry tackled the extremists' control over the curriculum that was being taught in schools spreading a culture of intolerance towards other cultures and religions. The Islamic studies curriculum was changed with more moderate interpretations of the Qur'an and more emphasis on research and sciences. The government initiated an extensive training program to upgrade the skills of educators, raise their level of awareness and instill in them the Muslim values of moderation and tolerance, which are the basic requirements for universal peace and prosperity.

Early childhood education has also become a top priority. The Ministry of education opened an average of one preschool per day in 2011 and there are plans to double this number.

The development of education or the *Tatweer* initiative was launched to improve nearly all aspects of education in the Kingdom, from teacher training through the quality of educational facilities to student-evaluation methods.

Extensive studies were conducted to upgrade the level of education and create a healthy environment in schools, colleges and universities. Academicians identified the main reasons behind the poor quality of education in schools and stressed the urgency to develop teaching styles rejecting the traditional method of rote learning. Students were not trained to have an opinion, and creativity was not encouraged; therefore, it was necessary to introduce training programs for teachers to implement innovative methods in teaching and using new techniques in the classrooms to support critical thinking and inspire students' creativity and enthusiasm. There are initiatives to introduce mentoring programs to build character and confidence, help students discover their capabilities and potentials and keep up to date with global developments.

Hopefully our school graduates with better educational standards will benefit more from their studies abroad and learn to be more respectful to other cultures in the world.

Seventeen public universities and 24 private colleges have been established, and they are encouraged by the Ministry to partner with foreign schools. Effat University, Dar Al-Hekma and private universities for girls that have maintained high education standards have partnered with several U.S. institutions, including Tufts ,the University of Miami, and Georgetown University among others. Others have followed suit. This type of international exchange has fostered cross-cultural understanding and empowered our graduates to meet the challenges of the 21st century.

Investing in education for women has been a priority of educational reforms. Women today represent almost 60percent of university graduates. Qualified women graduates continue to contribute greatly towards the country's national development. Vocational institutes for women have been introduced, and private colleges and universities for women have spread throughout major cities in the Kingdom facilitating the integration of more qualified women into the workforce.

Princess Nora bintAbdulRahman University, the first women's university in Saudi Arabia founded in 1970, has been expanded and modernized to accommodate 40,000 students and 12,000 employees. Today it is the largest women-only university in the world, and the most modern women's institution of higher education. It has fifteen colleges and several departments. The new Riyadh campus that openedin May 2011 has a 700-bed teaching hospital and research centers for nanotechnology, information technology and bioscience and other more traditional majors such as nursing and pharmacy.

The coming academic years will witness shifting male and female students to the integrated university campuses in Riyadh, Jeddah and Hasa that will provide an ideal environment for operation of the King Abdullah International Center for Medical Research, health centers and consultative studies center. So far a total of 227 students have graduated from the university.

Three major projects were reinforced to enhance creativity and excellence of faculty members, to promote the research culture and to raise the scientific level of students in Saudi universities nearer to international standards.

New universities were established in each region and a university branch was introduced in each governorate in order to provide all citizens better access to education. This development is very promising as it would guarantee an education for citizens in all regions of the Kingdom and provide them an opportunity for a better future.

Higher education was given priority as an essential means to develop human resources and build knowledgeable and skilled manpower to boost national development. Both the establishment of the National Center for Assessment in Higher Education in 2001 and the creation of the National Commission for Assessment of Academic Accreditation in 2004 were positive initiatives to ensure quality in the Kingdom's higher education system.

Three campuses of King Saud bin Abdul- Aziz University for Health Sciences are nearing completion. KSAU-HS will be the first public university in the Kingdom and the ME region specializing in health sciences.

There continues to be more awareness and significant support towards grants for scientific research projects and the establishment of technology incubators to contribute towards scientific and technological developments. King Abdullah University of Science and Technology offers doctoral degrees in chemical and biological engineering applied mathematics, environmental, chemical and computer science.

The proper implementation of these ambitious educational reforms will help our graduates contribute towards the development of their nation. The intent is that the qualifications our graduates acquire will ultimately solve the unemployment problem and boost the performance of the country's inadequate workforce.

The media continues to play a significant role in celebrating the achievements of young graduates who have obtained degrees from prestigious universities abroad and excelled in Saudi universities. Pictures of young women parading proudly in their graduation robes during ceremonies in universities abroad can hopefully present a more progressive picture of women in our society. Hopefully hardliners will get accustomed to see more examples of bright faces of women and recognize them as respected partners in the development of the nation.

King Abdullah Scholarship Program

The most significant achievement of King Abdullah is the scholarship program, which provided an opportunity for 120,000 students to study at universities abroad. The initiative was to raise the educational standard of Saudi graduates and expose a large number to other cultures promoting intercultural relations and peaceful coexistence.

The King Abdullah International Scholarship Program provides the means to pursue bachelor's, master's and doctorate degrees as well as medical fellowships in reputable universities around the world for example in the States, Britain, France, Germany China, Japan, India, Australia and Malaysia.

Students are directed to choose their majors according to market needs. Hopefully, the program will address the high rate of unemployment in the Kingdom, which is largely due to the poor academic standards of Saudi graduates and their lack of those skills required by the job market. Graduates are hoping to qualify for job opportunities in government ministries, national corporations and the private sector as well as the newly established universities, and the industrial cities in all regions of the Kingdom.

All government departments as well as the private sector are on a mission to accommodate and employ qualified Saudis. Their participation is greatly needed in the development of the nation.

The scholarship program also provides an opportunity for the students to build bridges of understanding and promote a cultural exchange that eradicate misconceptions between Saudi students and the rest of the world.

The program will enable students to learn from academic and scientific expertise and help them qualify in the various fields of study. The exchange and the experience will enhance the skills, and hopefully they will gain valuable experience to help them contribute to the nation's development.

Many Saudi students studying in the United States have performed exceedingly well in their studies and research. The interaction between students and their professors and the exposure of Saudi students to American work ethics and respect for knowledge has created a very positive impact on their academic performance.

Global standards that are applied in the American higher education system and the exchange between the students and US scholars were important aspects that energized the academic performance of the young postgraduate researchers and scientists. Hopefully the qualifications acquired

27

by these young graduates will help boost the performance of the country's underperforming workforce.

The King Abdullah International Scholarship Program includes many talented students whose innovative research has won recognition from some of the more distinguished American universities. Among them are three students who are working to help facilitate social and economic development in their country.

Hala Ridwan is among the most talented students. She is majoring in Political Science and History at Yale and is working on a civil code, *Almudawanah* Code, to serve women in her country who are abused and need to be protected by a codified law.

She began her research in 2011 after she learned how to apply analytical studies to come up with new conclusions in her methods of research class. Her professor recognized her talent in class and appointed her as research assistant.

Ridwan also attended a class in Islamic theology and worked on the reinterpretation of Islamic Shariah law. She conducted a study in which she analyzed the differences between family laws in Islamic countries and used her findings to create a civil code that could be applied in her country. In Morocco, she says, they base their law on the Maliki school of thought, and she hopes to apply it to the Hanbali school in order to adapt it to Saudi laws and tradition.

Ridwan represents the new generation of Saudi students who are both well qualified and eager to serve their community and contribute toward a better society.

Ahmed Al-Fares is a fellowship student at Harvard. He scored the highest ranking among all the fellows in clinical molecular genetics. Harvard awarded him a research grant to develop and design programs for DNA testing at the university. He has been working on his research since earning his earlier degree from McGill University in Montreal.

Al-Fares spoke about the encouragement and support provided in Canadian and American universities with mentors and experts in the field providing full assistance with extreme flexibility that encourages researchers to excel. He and his colleagues consequently succeeded in detecting a gene with a new technology called the next generation sequence. His research has been published in international journals and Al-Fares hopes that physicians and scientists will get the same kind of support, so they can conduct research that can save lives and help patients in his country.

Ahmed Al-Ghazi is a student at Santa Clara University. He is studying production mechanical systems design, and is working on an innovative project called *Goom* to develop an apparatus that will enable the handicapped and elderly to move independently.

He is also producing a YouTube program to encourage young Saudis to be more innovative and to look for solutions to prevalent problems and find ways to use technology to serve the community. His idea came to him when he realized his grandmother's frustration because she was always dependent on others to cater to her needs.

Al-Ghazi has been encouraged by his university teachers to continue his innovative project. He says that both leading investors encouraged him, and companies specialized in medical technology showed an interest in funding his research. He added that was proud to be a part of the King Abdullah Scholarship Program and intends to register his patent in his own country. He hopes the results of his research and development will be on the market within a year or two.

Dr. Mohammed Al-Eissa, the Saudi Cultural Attaché in Washington, is the progressive leader who is behind the great success of the King Abdullah Scholarship Program in the US. He heads a mission of 400 employees all dedicated to serving the interests of almost 80,000 students across the US. Dr. Al-Eissa could write books about his experience and efforts that have helped many students adapt to living in America and achieving academic success.

The expectations of the young Saudi graduates are very high. It would be a real disappointment if they were not received with the same kind of encouragement and respect that America and the Saudi Cultural Mission have offered them in the United States and in other advanced universities in other parts of the world

It would also be a great shame if Government departments and the private sector fail to pave the way for integrating these qualified graduates into the job market in order to enhance the standards of the workforce. The new generation will not accept it if they are not provided with the opportunities they deserve. The prevalent bureaucracy and inefficiency still needs to be addressed in order to serve the needs of the thousands of graduates returning home after a journey of intellectual freedom and global awareness.

Chapter 3

Human Rights in Saudi Arabia

The concept of human rights and the rights of women in Islam have been issues of great concern to many in the Kingdom and abroad. It is very unfortunate that not many Saudis are aware of their rights and responsibilities. As a result there is little respect for law and order. Traffic laws are broken, financial rights abused, citizens' rights neglected and women's rights unrecognized.

A recent study released by the National Society of Human Rights revealed that 94 percent of Saudi society does not have any knowledge of human rights laws, and 50 percent believe that the spread of the human rights culture in the Kingdom is still very weak. The study showed that 40 percent of the victims of violence were unwilling to lodge a complaint to human rights authorities, and 53 percent did not resort to any appropriate authority after being subjected to violence or abuse.

The study showed that of the five regions in Saudi Arabia the Eastern Province is most aware of the concept of human rights at 65 percent, while the Northern region is the least aware at 46 percent. What is most interesting about the study is that women have a better knowledge of human rights than men, yet they remain silent.

The report prompted an immediate response from King Abdullah, who issued a directive to pursue a plan to boost the culture of human rights and introduce human-rights education in Saudi schools.

Moreover, members of the Shoura Council supported the study. Dr.Ibrahim Al- Shiddi, chairman of the Human Rights and Complaints committee at the Shoura Council told reporters that he did not find the percentages strange or astonishing and agreed that human rights awareness in the Kingdom is clearly very weak. He stressed the need to implement King Abdullah's directive to spread awareness about human rights among Saudi citizens. He also urged the Ministry of Education to include the subject of human rights in the school curriculum to teach the new generation the culture of human rights.

Dr.SuhailaZainAlabideen, who is a board member of the National Society for Human Rights (NSHR), is vice president of the Studies and Consultations Committee and the Scientific Committee. She holds that there has been positive progress on human rights taking place in Saudi Arabia. "We are moving on the right path as a result of the acceptance and understanding of human rights, where every member of the family has a right to a good life based on Islamic values," she said.

Dr.Alabideenmaintains that it is the responsibility of the entire Muslim world to clear the distorted interpretations of some verses of the holy Quran and the Sunnah. Her dream is to straighten out the mistakes about religious discourse. Dr.Alabideen is a prominent advocate of women's rights in Saudi Arabia. Her eloquence and scholarly knowledge of Shariah law gives her the authority to debate controversial issues concerning the legal rights of women in Islam. She has appeared on numerous talk shows and has given many radio and television interviews speaking out against the discrimination of women in the name of Islam.

Dr.Alabideen defends the right of Muslim women to take leadership positions. She asserts that men should accept working under the leadership of a woman and that qualified women have a right to participate in the decision-making process just as they used to do in the days of the Prophet, may peace be upon Him.

There are plans to lift the ban on the appearance of women lawyers in courtrooms. Currently women attorneys still cannot appear in court or police stations in order to argue a case. They can only work in an office doing legal consultation or study court cases and draft legal notices.

There are more than 1,500 women attorneys, 1,000 of them studied abroad under the King AbdullahScholarship Program. Others have graduated from law and Shariah specializations at seven colleges and universities across the Kingdom since 2008.

This increasing number of women law graduates has pressured the government to lift the ban and to allow women lawyers to practice their profession. Moreover, the increasing numbers of women lawyers boosted the profession and supported the earlier graduates of British, American and Egyptian universities.

Women law graduates were shown great encouragement by royalty in Riyadh, and they were given prominent coverage in the local press, highlighting the importance of their role in ensuring justice for the divorced and the physically abused women in society.

One of the most promising initiatives taken to empower the law graduates was the opening of a training program in legal counselling. The program was initiated by Princess Sarah Bint Musaad Bin Abdul Aziz, chairwoman of the board of directors of the MawadahFoundation.

The objectives of the program are mainly to address the negative effects of divorce and to raise the efficiency of justice in marital and family cases, training women lawyers in court deliberations, and above all, promoting the culture of human rights in family issues.

The four-month course was an introduction to personal status cases, including alimony, custody rights, visitation and inheritance. It also included lessons in communication skills, how to deal with pressure, building self-confidence and preparation of legal petitions.

The Alwaleed Bin Talal foundation also donated SR726,000 to the MawadahFoundation to help support 500 women law graduates.

The foundation aims to reduce the very high divorce rate in the Kingdom by raising public awareness of the importance of families for social stability, addressing the negative aspects of broken homes and supporting women going through a divorce.

Women law graduates continue to gain more support in society and are being mentored and given special care by officials and the Justice Department. It is only a matter of time before they will appear in court and before Saudi judges to represent their clients in police stations and criminal investigations.

Protecting Human Rights

Some members of the Commission for the Promotion of Virtue and Discouragement of Vice (*Hai'a*) violate Islamic religious teachings when they abuse the rights of citizens. They act under the distorted principle that every individual is guilty until proven innocent and disregard the universal principle that every individual is innocent until proven guilty. They want to impose aberrant customs and traditions and refuse to respect people who wish to adopt a more modern lifestyle labelling it as unIslamic.

There is growing public frustration over the inability to control the continued violations by Commission staff members. Some incidents are reported by the media, but many others are never revealed because people are either afraid to report them or are unaware of their rights.

The government has issued reassurances and officials in the Ministry of Justice have been promising to curb the authority of Commission staff members. In some cases a few have been publicly reprimanded or given mild sentences; however, the violations still continue, and people been have been injured and abused, and some have died.

The media reported that a citizen in Baha was killed, and his wife and two children were injured when their car, which was reportedly being chased by a Commission patrol vehicle, fell off a bridge that was under construction. The woman, who was five months pregnant, sustained severe contusions and abrasions, and the couple's son was in hospital in critical condition. The deceased's brother said the family was picnicking at a park when they were approached by a member of the Commission staff who complained that their car stereo was too loud. The deceased and the Commission staffer argued for a while, and when the family left, a Commission vehicle chased the family car until it got to the bridge.

There is a dire need to educate the members of the public and spread awareness about their rights. There is a need to put into action a plan that honors the rights of citizens and protect them from further abuse.

The media should be encouraged to address the subject. The subject should be introduced in schools, and debates should be held to raise awareness and correct misconceptions about Islamic principles that have been improperly imposed. It is our responsibility to clear up the distorted interpretations and address the mistakes prevalent in religious discourse. It is no longer acceptable for hardliners to take advantage of the ignorance of innocent people and impose their extreme doctrine on law-abiding citizens who do not violate Islamic principles but do not agree with the restrictions of Commission regulations.

Housing Rights

"Housing is a basic human right and one of the basic requirements for an honorable life." So said an official statement by the, deputy chairman of the National Society for Human Rights (NSHR). According to the latest report released by the NSHR, "a large number of citizens cannot afford to buy a home due to the increase in real estate prices." Officials of the society urged that, "housing allowances should be paid to citizens who do not satisfy the criteria for owning a house set by the Ministry of Housing"

The housing problem has been left unsolved for a long time. It represents a national challenge that will be difficult to address due to the speed at which the Kingdom's population is growing. Expanding public services to meet the demands of the growing population will continue to be a major challenge that will require more serious attention.

According to recent statistics, only 30 percent of Saudis own homes. Immediate measures must be implemented to provide all Saudis with the opportunity to live a life of dignity and honor if the government is serious about implementing reforms.

The government has announced plans for massive housing projects at a cost of over SR300 billion, and aggressive development projects have been initiated all over the country. Many international companies and property developers have been encouraged to invest in the Saudi construction sector.

Meanwhile, the General Organization for Pensions has given approval for the implementation of housing projects in Riyadh, Jeddah and Dammam. Despite these concerted efforts, senior officials warn that further programming, management and coordination are needed to prevent problems from arising. Indeed, it is crucial at this stage to apply international standards and to ensure respect for laws and regulations so that these plans are implemented rapidly and efficiently.

The enormity of the problem and the continued public discontent makes it unforgivable to allow the dreams of Saudis to be shattered by the poor standards and reckless planning of inefficient workers and incompetent managers who waste valuable government resources.

The housing sector was neglected for a long time. Government laws and regulations were not enforced to implement proper urban planning or to establish the needed infrastructure before housing construction begins. Currently there is no main sewerage in the city, and roads have to be torn up to put in pipes to serve each new house, which disturbs the residents of every neighbourhood and affects the commercial and social life of the city.

At present public utilities are lacking, and there is no supervision to implement the necessary services to avoid the chaos that existed in the past. The proper distribution of residential and commercial areas is not planned to respect the privacy and comfort of residents.

There is a lack of close cooperation between the municipality, housing developers and the construction companies involved. There is no well-planned symmetry in the architecture and landscape design orcolor scheme that reflects the culture.

"There is a global initiative to address the perceived challenge of global warming. Environmentally friendly development underlies many nations' development policies yet in Saudi Arabia there are no serious efforts to build houses that are environmentally friendly. Sustainable housing has been discouraged because of the public perception that it is expensive, and people are unaware of the long-term financial benefits, mainly reducing the cost of water and electricity, that are burdensfor all at the end of every month.

Lately housing specialists have stepped up a campaign to introduce new concepts of sustainable development. Local government should study these concepts and involve citizens in the process of planning sustainable programs that can address the environmental challenges of extreme heat and the scarcity of water. Potential methods that can be applied to implement sustainable housing, which include, site design, passive solar design, natural light and ventilation, are non- existent. Both lack of proper building codes and the unplanned distribution of residential areas have been a source of public discontent. Many family residential areas have turned into commercial centers creating security risks and depriving citizens of comfort and privacy. High-rise developments, shopping malls, schools and mosques should have their own parking lots and should be strategically located so as not to disturb the harmony of the neighborhood.

The interests of citizens should be considered before the implementation of any public service. Plans need to be applied according to updated research to help us avoid earlier mistakes, and municipalitiesneed tolearn from the experience of more developed nations. Unfortunately global standards were compromised, and officials have been negligent in serving public interests.

The National Human Rights Society has now called for urgent measures to address the rights of citizens to own their own homes, and the Ministry of Housing has allocated a large budget for housing projects. The public is now waiting with anticipation for the final outcome and hoping that government officials can expedite housing projects to meet the demands of all the people.

Human Rights Policies Delayed

Evidently one of the many reasons why reformers have had little success in influencing change is the half-hearted approach of policymakers to embrace modernity with progressive strategies and better initiatives to effect change and development. They remain reluctant to confront powerful extremists elements in society.

Moreover, the conventional policy of authoritarian constraint did not permit the implementation of flexible programs to ensure basic rights for all citizens. Rather it allowed the influence of negative and un-progressive attitudes to exist depriving many of the freedom to progress and excel.

The social attitude of many segments in society, who are convinced that there is no urgency for domestic reform, is the main obstacle to progress. There are many who are persuaded that we need to develop slowly to allow society more time to accept change and adopt more progressive attitudes. What they fail to realize is that the delay will add more hurdles, and the challenges will continue to grow more complex. We live in an era of increasing economic pressure. The pace of global progress is accelerating, and the acknowledgement of global competitiveness is not so much a concern as an imperative for survival.

The slow implementation of human-rights policies and the weak attempts to enforce judicial and organizational reforms make it difficult to build the effective citizenship that is essential for a modern day society.

The inadequate provisions for basic human needs to ensure a better life, such as public transportation, job opportunities, health services, school facilities, public parks and proper housing to accommodate a burgeoning population, pose a major threat to the social stability and progress of the country. Corruption, bureaucracy and incompetent employees also stand in the way of implementing vital reforms. Valuable time is wasted, and government money is not utilized efficiently. Poor governance needs to be addressed, and the traditional management system needs to be modernized. The old school of a centralized system must be upgraded with management that delegates work to qualified personnel who can get the work done without delay. The lack of incentives and low wages are behind the poor productivity in many government departments. There is a need to raise awareness about work ethics and global standards of quality and productivity in order to influence change and provide better services to all of the nation's people. The government should work harder on training young Saudis and upgrading their skills. Policy makers need to understand that the proportion of Saudis employed is not necessarily as important as the efficiency and effectiveness of those employed.

The way to catch up with global progress is to activate a vibrant civil society that can complement government policies, push the implementation of laws and promote the skills of citizenship essential for a more tolerant and progressive environment. Civil society development, however, is being constrained by legal structures that preclude the formation of civil institutions and non-governmental organizations. Currently the law requires all welfare societies to register under a central authority, and highly restrictive procedures are imposed to ban the activities of civic groups eager to address social issues such as labor rights or gender equality.

Discrimination against women and the Guardianship rule

The guardianship rule is a major violation of human rights and an impediment to progress and reform. According to the latest official statistics of 2012, women constitute half of our population and 57 percent of our university graduates. A report issued by Khadija Bint Khuwailed Business Center stated that Saudi women owned about 20,000 small-, medium- and large-scale companies and firms with a total capital of about SR100 billion.

Yet half of our population remains shackled by the imposed guardianship law that perpetuates injustice and discrimination against women. Even a matter as basic as physical exercise — an essential for good health — becomes an issue in the current state of affairs. Women are struggling to fight discrimination in the courts because many judges and senior members of the *Ulama* are either unaware or indifferent to their suffering. Women have no voice in the council of senior scholars or as advisers to the grand mufti to address their needs and grievances. They have no say in decisions that affect their lives and their families —unacceptable treatment for women in the modern era.

Economists stress that the high cost of living and inflation make it difficult for single-income families to provide the basic needs for the average family living in Saudi Arabia today. The participation of women in the work force is no longer a luxury; it has become an economic necessity. Unfortunately, women represent only 16 percent of the total work force, which reflects a very high unemployment rate among women. Job opportunities for women are limited, and the bellicose, unreasoned societal pushback against women in leadership positions often erodes what little progress is made to project the true principles of Islam that honor women and protect their rights.

Princess Adela, the King's daughter and wife of Minister of Education Prince Faisal Bin Abdullah who also heads the Home Healthcare Society, supports the campaign for women's empowerment. During a two-day forum on the "Participation of Women in the National Economy," the Princess gave a reasoned presentation in which she urged a greater role for women in the nation's development. "The participation of women in the national development faces many challenges because of tradition," the princess said. "It is still below expectations. There is an urgent need for Saudi Arabia to diversify its activities and balance economic growth with population growth. With 25 percent of the Saudi society financially helping the other 75 percent, a greater role for women in social development cannot be over emphasized."

Discrimination against women in the name of Islam and the hard-line position adopted by some Saudi women does not help their image in other Muslim countries. The religious message of the hard-liners who exert great control over the society is unacceptable to other Muslims around the world who adhere to other Islamic schools of thought. Across the Muslim world, women vote and run in national elections, and they sometimes lead their nations. Even GCC countries with societies similar to our own have recognized women in leadership positions. Women in Bahrain and Kuwait have become ministers; in Oman they are active members of the Shoura Council. The rest of the Arab world has many women leaders who have been active as legislators and legal participants in the decision-making process. Saudi Arabia has yet to modernize and support its own women leaders and legislators.

The country needs to address still more challenges. The confrontation between the moderates and the hardliners has reached a critical stage. Government support for both hardliners and the moderates will create two extremes at a parallel level causing a serious threat to national social stability.

The Commission for the Promotion of Virtue and the Prevention of Vice, the *Hai'a*, was a barrier standing in the way of reform and continues to be a source of public discontent. The organization is a symbol of intolerance, and its members show no respect for the public, encouraging people to spy on everyone and instigating others to be their informants , harassing women on the streets over the type of Abaya or wearing makeup in malls. The government is also to blame for allowing their abusive behavior and providing them with legal and financial support. They have legal authority and are always accompanied and protected by the police. They keep a distance at times, but they soon intrude harassing women and children in the malls. One of the very disturbing practices was stopping couples to check identification cards and questioning their relationship and arresting them if they are not legally married. After public uproar that practice was stopped.

Many of the young have become disillusioned by the failure of both the reformers and hardliners and hence adopted an extremely negative attitude against their values and traditions. The fear factor among the young is diminishing, and their faith in their elders and educators is at risk. This is a dangerous situation that warns of potential chaos and possibly violent behavior from a frustrated and growing percentage of the population.

Chapter 4

IMPORTANT STEPS TOWARD MODERNIZING SAUDI ARABIA

1. Women in The Shoura and Municipal Councils,
2. Can Political involvement of women influence change?
3. Women in leadership positions
4. An obligation to act as role models
5. Women's campaigns influence change
6. Status of women corrected
7. Cultural contributions
8. Popular Philanthropy
9. Women in sports
10. A Bedtime story
11. A Ministry for Women's Affairs

Women in The Shoura and Municipal Councils

The first serious step towards modernizing Saudi Arabia was the decision finally to allow women to run and vote in municipal elections and become members of the Shoura Council. Women will be allowed to vote and run in Municipal elections in 2015, and they are now official members of the Shoura Council . The announcement came on Sept. 26, 2011, a significant date long to be remembered. Although the four-year delay to Shoura membership was somewhat disappointing for many, the majority of women were optimistic and looked forward to their future participation in public life. This development will bring a positive change that would finally end an era of discrimination against women. The Custodian of the Two Holy Mosques King Abdullah will go down in history as the reformer who paved the way for progress in Saudi Arabia.

In his inaugural speech at the third year of the Shoura Council's fifth session, King Abdullah rejected any marginalization of women in any domain and encouraged their participation, citing the examples of prominent women in the history of Islam. "All people know the role of women in the annals of Islam, and their positions cannot be marginalized," he said.

This was a statement that showed his determination to empower women and end any attempt to undermine their role in the name of Islam. It demonstrated a firm stand against people who were resistant to change and against the empowerment of women in Saudi Arabia.

Discrimination against women in society and the consequent restrictions imposed on them are the two main factors that have slowed progress in this country. In his speech, King Abdullah recognized the need to modernize and spoke against those who opposed progressive thinking and were reluctant to give women their due rights. He defied the hard-liners who have been obstacles on the path to a better future.

"Balanced modernization in line with Islamic values, which preserve rights, is an important requirement in an era with no place for the weak and people with indecisiveness," he said. The monarch called on Saudi citizens, both men and women, to ask for their rights and achieve their goals with dignity. He openly attacked those who reject reforms and welcomed the participation of all citizens in the decision-making process.

He also warned those who were arrogant and defied moderate Shariah guidelines that they would have to bear the consequences of their negative positions. "My brothers and sisters, you have your own rights according to

Islamic law to achieve your goals with pride and dignity," he said. "It is our right to seek your opinion and advice according to Shariah guidelines and the fundamentals of religion, and those who stay away from these guidelines are arrogant people, and they have to bear the responsibility for their actions".

The new royal decision to include women in the Shoura Council and ensure their participation in municipal elections was received with great joy and jubilation across the country. It reflected a major recognition of their capabilities and qualifications and a political decision to change the negative attitudes of society toward them. The country could be witnessing a new beginning that will usher in positive attitudes and create a healthier environment, where children will have the opportunity to grow in an atmosphere of hope and enlightenment; young women will be inspired by the success of their mothers and sisters, and young men will learn to respect the role of women as professionals and equal partners.

It is such a relief that the demands of the educated elite among Saudi women have finally been granted. They will at last be given the opportunity to speak on behalf of women who are oppressed and underprivileged. They will be able to address women's issues and motivate women to become active citizens who can help society advance and prosper.

The task ahead is very challenging. Women in decision-making positions must now live up to the expectations of both the King and the whole country. As members of the Shoura and municipal councils they will be required to outline the challenges that have slowed progress, and identify the policies that have undermined their role and contributions towards the welfare of society.

Negative attitudes exist against women as a result of the influence of hardliners, who continue to impose their distorted Islamic rulings and use rigid interpretations of Islamic concepts to support their baseless ideas.

However, the presence of women in the Shoura Council can now effect changes and allow them to call for new policies in order to radically improve the status of women in this society. The appointment of women in the Shoura and municipal councils will enable them to exercise pressure on hardliners and confront the challenges that have hindered their progress. Chief among these are: the reluctance to support women in leadership positions, the "legal guardianship" rule, the strict culture of segregation within society, the discriminatory policies and the opposition to women driving. Women Shoura Councillors will be in a position to serve the interests of working women, for example pushing for adequate maternity leave, reasonable working hours, onsite workplace nurseries and equal pay.

These women will have a responsibility to identify and reject laws and regulations that are incompatible with women's needs in today's world. The need for a codified system to ensure a uniform application of Shariah law is a major demand. Women in Shoura are expected to call for the elimination of laws governing legal guardianship, and to address the injustices in cases of extreme jail sentences, floggings, child marriages, domestic abuse, child custody and divorce on grounds of tribal incompatibility.

As official members of Shoura Council they could facilitate the participation of qualified and professional women in governmental and managerial positions thus allowing them to have a say in decisions that affect their lives and the lives of their children. They are expected to promote the activities of civil society and adopt the causes of women who suffer discrimination. This way they can help decision makers face on-the-ground realities.

The role of women in the Shoura Council should not merely be an honorary one if government is serious about reforms and social justice. The only way to guarantee their effective role is by advising all government departments to respect their participation as experts and opinion leaders representing the whole society and not just the marginalized half of the Saudi population. Representatives must always remember that they have a responsibility to speak for all citizens' rights in every sphere of national life and a duty to extend professional advice to achieve social reforms and economic prosperity for all.

The decision to allow the full participation of women in nation building is a bold step in the right direction. Today we can safely say that the first step in the long journey on the road to progress has finally been taken. Excluding women from leadership positions and not taking into account their opinions on major decisions that affect their lives was a source of frustration to many.

Social activists believe that the challenges facing women are overwhelming. Prominent columnists including Aziza Almanie, BadriaAlbishr, Hatoon Al-Fassi, FawziaAlbakr and Samar Almigrin, have written many articles about the lack of proper services and of basic requirements for a better life, mainly public transportation, job opportunities, health services and the discrimination against women in the workplace. The spread of the ultra-conservative *Salafi* doctrine in the region has strengthened the influence of extremists who are against the empowerment of women and their participation in public life. It might take a generation or two to influence change and correct the status of women across Saudi society; however, the new members of the Shoura can expedite the process of reforms and provide the next generation of women with more opportunities for a better future.

King Abdullah's vision to revise the status of women has endeared him to all the women in Saudi Arabia. He has reiterated on many occasions his support for the integration of women into the work force and welcomed their contributions to achieve economic and social prosperity. Now he has crowned his reform movement with the decision to include them in public life.

Can Political Involvement of Women Influence Change?

The participation of women in the Shoura Council will certainly end an era of discrimination against women and promote their integration into the political and social process. Thirty distinguished women with impressive credentials have at last been nominated to become official members of the Shoura Council with equal rights as their male counterparts. Hopefully they will have enough confidence to stand up for the rights of the underprivileged, and they will be able to effectively address many issues that need urgent attention to help our nation prosper and develop.

As officials of the advisory body that reports directly to the King, they need to take advantage of their position to boldly address domestic challenges and come up with effective recommendations for new policies and scientific solutions to create a better environment for our fast growing younger generation, mainly unemployment, housing, transportation, health services and many other issues that are keeping us behind the more advanced countries of the world.

Previously the council had 12 women advisers who were only consulted on matters related to women, families and children andtheir presence wasnot very effective. Todaythe public expects much more from the new members who will have equal rights to engage in transparent debates with their male counterparts in the council.

Women in Saudi Arabia today will finally have a voice in government. They will be given the opportunity to outline recommendations for better State policies and innovative strategies to implement reforms.

It is unfortunate that thereare many sceptics who doubt the role of women in the council. They continue to question their effectiveness and their ability to influence change. It is equally depressing to be confronted withhardliners who reject the presence of women there. They have already started their campaign against them and are openly protesting their membership in the shoura, calling it un-Islamic.

Meanwhilethe progressive and the professionals are more hopeful and are eager to support the political involvement of women and trust their ability to support King Abdullah's reform movement and affect change in Saudi Arabia.

The participation of women in the Shoura faces many challenges. Segregation restrictions are already a topic of public debate. It is unclear how the council will debate issues with women members.The government has announced that the Shoura Council women will have equal rights as the men, however they will have separate entrances and separate quarters and they have been assigned women employees to facilitate a segregated work environment. Many professional women view this segregated policy as a form of discrimination and are disappointed by the implementation of the rigid policy that could limit the role of women in the council.

However the majority of Saudi women are optimistic and they are all united in their support for the chosen women in the shoura and look forward to further participations of women in public life.

The media must exert greater efforts to raisenational awareness about their political role and encourage the new parliamentary experience among women in Saudi Arabia.

The experienced women in the council are expected to promote the activities of civil society to help decision makers face ground realities.Their participation in the decision making process will enable them to confront discriminatory policies against women.The women in the shoura will be in a stronger position to influence recommendations that are submitted directly to the King. It remains to be seen how effective they will be. The chosen experts have been honoured with this post to serve the interests of all citizensThey have gained the trust of the King and public expectations are high. They must not allow obstructionists to stand in the way of progress and enlightenment.

Women in LeadershipPositions

At this critical stage of modernizing Saudi Arabia, it is important to identify potential leaders who can be challenged to come up with new initiatives to implement King Abdullah's ambitious reforms. Putting the right man or woman in the right place is the key to success. However, this has not been the case in some government departments and institutions. Unfortunately, not many people put into leadership positions are blessed with leadership qualities. As a result many promised reforms have not been delivered; money has been wasted, and efforts exerted have all been in vain.

Capable leaders are people who have progressive characters, command respect so that when they speak, others listen; are committed and able to deliver no matter what, and are mentally tough enough to take criticism and learn from their mistakes. Not many Saudi officials have these qualities that would revive trust in government initiatives and accordingly they have failed to accelerate the needed reforms to help the country change and modernize. However there are those who are trying hard to influence change and progress.

The Deputy Minister of Education Nora Al-Fayez recently met King Abdullah Scholarship students studying in the United States and succeeded in demonstrating that she is an official who is capable of upgrading the education system to transform the Kingdom into a knowledge-based society. She was the first woman to attain such a high governmental rank in Saudi Arabia. Initially she was a disappointment. Her earlier image of a woman in a black *niqab*(veil) refusing to allow her pictures in the Saudi press presented a distorted image of the progressive and highly educated graduate of Utah State University, which recently granted her an honorary doctorate degree for her leading role in serving the women of her country.

Nora Al-Fayez in her elegant and colorful hijab presented an ideal role model for young Saudi men and women. The official met the students of both genders in an informal and flexible environment — not through the traditional and frequently used closed-circuit TV. It was an excellent opportunity for the students to see her in person and learn about her initiatives and progressive ideas. She commanded respect and was very inspiring in her remarks to the students.

Addressing the failures of the Saudi educational system, she said, "The process of reforms has to take its due course," and stressed the need to build capacity and spread social awareness in order to ensure the proper implementation of effective reforms across the nation. The discussion with the students was very transparent, and it demonstrated the extent of their maturity and awareness. A postgraduate education major explained how she was embarrassed in class because she was the only one who knew nothing about the First and Second World Wars. She was critical of the curriculum and the unqualified teachers who continue to teach in the Kingdom.

Another student compared safety measures in American schools with the inappropriate safety measures in Saudi schools, which have led to fires endangering the lives of many innocent children across the Kingdom. The introduction of physical education in girls' schools and the lack of proper sports facilities in public schools, the lack of preschool nurseries and nursery facilities for school teachers, the failure of parents to participate in school activities and the failure of schools to build character in students were also among the topics of discussion.

After a long discussion, the deputy minister welcomed the students' observations and urged them to share their recommendations through the ministry's website. She explained that reforms are taking place but that it will take time to build the capacity of the workforce and the infrastructure needed to achieve the desired goals. However, she said that she was hopeful that within 10 years Saudi Arabia would witness the positive effects of the reform initiatives.

Dr. Samar Al-Saggaf, head of the Department of Medical Health Sciences Programs at the Saudi Cultural Mission, is another official with leadership qualities. She has been instrumental in identifying the great potential of Saudi medical students and has inspired many to excel and achieve greater success. Medical students in the program all testify to her leadership qualities. Dr. Al-Saggaf is also an Associate Professor at King Abdulaziz University, and was the former Dean of the Women's Section where she served to promote women's education.

Indeed the leadership qualities of these officials are the main reasons behind their accomplishments.

Unfortunately, there are other officials who have failed to demonstrate such qualities. They have insisted on maintaining the status quo and have neither offered any solutions to prevalent problemsnor have been willing to take on the burden of responsibility. They seem to lack motivation and are hindered by their egocentric attitudes.

Saudi youth today will not accept leadership by the incompetent; they will refuse to continue to lag behind the more advanced countries of the world. The only way the government can restore the trust of the young is by appointing the more capable and qualified leaders who can help citizens meet the challenges of the 21st century.

An obligation to Act as Role Models

According to the latest report published by UNESCO, 40 percent of Saudi doctors are women. In the field of science and research there is an increasing number of successful women who have earned global recognition and have inspired many Saudi women today.

Dr.Khawla Al Kurai, chief cancer researcher at King Fahd Research Center is among the youngest and most distinguished doctors in her field. She has won international awards for her distinguished research in the field of medicine. She is on the board of editors of BMC "Genomica," a well-known journal on genetics. Dr. Al Kurai has participated in manynational and international conferences and has been instrumental in highlighting the new image of Saudi women doctors and scientists in her country and abroad. She has also been nationally recognized by King Abdullah for her academic achievements and scientific contributions.

Professor Samira Islam, the head of the Drug Monitoring Unit at the King Fahd Research Center, has made significant contributions in drug safety by defining the Saudi profile for drug metabolism. She has held several academic leadership posts in Saudi Arabia as well as international diplomatic posts within The World Health Organization. She has also contributed significantly in the Saudi educational system for girls. UNESCO nominated Prof. Islam as the first distinguished Arab Muslim scientist in the world for the year 2000. She has held academic leadership positions in Saudi Arabia and abroad. Dr. Islam has worked hard to build the academic infrastructure to support women studying science in the Saudi higher education system.

Dr.Maha Al Muneef,Executive Director of the National Family Safety Program and councillor of the International Society for the Prevention of Child Abuse and Neglect, is a child protectionist and child rights advocate. She is also a consultant on pediatric infectious diseases and has been involved in the national implementation of child protection services. She is chairwoman of Suspected Child Abuse and Neglect Center at the King Abdul Aziz Medical City, a fellow of the American Pediatrics association and President-elect of the Arab Professional Network for the Prevention of Violence Against Children. She is also a consultant to the Shoura Council. Dr.Almuneef has dedicated her career to prevent child abuse and raise public awareness about the need to address the social problem and train doctors to recognize the victims of abuse and neglect. She also called for legal action against child molesters.

Dr.Almuneef started the National SafetyProgram in 1999 with her colleagues to address the abuse of women and children by husbands and fathers and was supported by the patronage of Princess Adela, the daughter of King Abdullah. Dr.Muneef worked hard to educate women about their legal rights, and she offered legal and social assistance to the victims who were usually unable to escape from an abusive home. She was also instrumental in establishing centers to protect the victims. She campaigned in many parts of the Kingdom to raise awareness and succeeded in organizing three significant symposiums,in Jeddah, Medina and Abha, which were instrumental in enacting the country's first laws criminalizing violence against women and children

In order to address the bias attitude within the judiciary the Dr.Almuneef engaged judges, lawyers, police officers and activists to protect the rights of women and children and expose the unjust and un-Islamic criminal acts of abusive husbands and fathers.

With the royal support of Princess Adela, Dr.Almuneef succeeded in educating the public about the rights of women and children and exposed the fallacies of the biased judiciary condoning cruelty against women

The Executive Director of National Family Protection Program,Dr. MahaAlmuneef, has activated one of the most effective reform programs ever to serve Saudi justice, humanity and society..

The success of these distinguished women has undoubtedly boosted the morale of those who were once abused and marginalized. There are some who have reached leadership positions and many others who have an obligation to act as role models for future generations. Women doctors, scientists and researchers are expected to contribute towards a socially, politically and economically progressive nation.

The Status of women corrected

Professional women continue to show great courage and determination to dispel the stereotypes of Saudi women as being oppressed and uneducated. They continue to project a new image and have succeeded in asserting their progressive identities on the world stage.

Qualified women today say they can no longer remain marginalized and confined to limited professions. Their contributions reflect their capabilities in new fields of specializations previously limited to them such as banking and finance,information technology and consultancy.

Gaining the confidence of the business community through discipline and hard work, they serve as board members, CEOs and consultants in many companies and organizations. Today there are many examples of highly qualified women who continue to promote innovative businesses and enterprises and are taking an active role in shaping the Saudi economy and introducing women into the business community.

Among them are: NahedTaher, CEO and co-founder of Gulf One Investment Bank, who was listed among the 20 most influential people in Islamic finance by the global Islamic Finance Magazine in 2012. In 2005 she became the first woman to head a Saudi investment bank in the Gulf Region. In 2006 she was ranked 72nd on the list of the 100 most powerful women in the world. She says Saudi women can play a larger role in developing the economy and advises them to invest more in their country. Taher remains a pioneer in the banking business, portraying a positive image of Saudi women in the international business community.

Lama Alsolaiman, deputy chairwoman of the Jeddah Chamber Of Commerce and Industry, was thefirst Saudi woman to be elected to this post in 2009. She is a board member of the Jeddah-based Rolaco Trading and Contracting Co., the National Institute of Health Services and the Economic and Social Circle of the Makkah Region. She was ranked fifth on the list of the 100 most powerful Arab women in 2011. She has effectively used her position to empower women in business and provide them the confidence and support to succeed in a male-dominated environment.

NashwaTaher was one of the first Saudi women to be elected as a board member in the Jeddah Chamber Of Commerce and Industry, (JCCI). Taher was ranked 59th on the list of the 100 most powerful women in the Arab World in 2011. She is currently an active member of the JCCI and vice president of The Khadija Bint Khuwailed Business Center for Women.

Taher continues to be a strong advocate for women in business. She has supported many women entrepreneurs and has called for new laws and regulations to support women at work and in business.

Dr. Arwa Alama is the first woman to hold a senior post in the Jeddah Municipality. She became the head of the IT Department there in 2008. Dr. Alama has played a great role in the country's technological advancement and has won her IT department eight prestigious awards. She also holds the position of vice mayor for Women's Affairs and has been instrumental in opening new job opportunities for women in municipal services. Dr. Alama is an associate professor in the Department of Computer Science at King Abdul Aziz University and has trained and encouraged many women in the IT sector. She is an IT consultant for Savola International and member of several scientific computer work groups, including the executive committee for the eGoverment Plan and the Saudi National Science and Technology Plan.

These women are but a few of the professional women who have been instrumental in helping to correct the status of women within Saudi society. It is crucial at this critical stage of modernizing the Kingdom, to step up a more aggressive campaign at the grass roots level to raise the awareness among citizens about the valuable contributions of professional women towards the progress of their society.

Highly qualified and talented women are beginning to gradually gain recognition by large businesses and government departments today. Their dedication and enthusiasm have contributed to their success and will hopefully lead to their full integration into the workforce. There are signs of decreasing resistance by conservative families to allow women to work, and a large segment of society has welcomed their participation in many fields that were taboo in the past.

Women represent almost 60 percent of the university graduates in Saudi Arabia. The government has gradually accepted the inclusion of women in the decision-making process. The presence of women on the Shoura Council could certainly influence change and accelerate much needed social economic and political reforms. Professional women today are eager to take on this role, and many have already started lobbying for their membership and are building expertise to qualify for political participation. Others are getting ready to run for elections and preparing for their participation in the electoral process, raising public awareness and civic responsibility.

Women's Campaigns Influence Change

Women activists played a great role in mobilizing the national base towards social change and prompting the government's decision to allow the participation of women in the Shoura and the municipal councils. The *Baladi* campaign, led by Dr.Nayla Attar, a business consultant, called for women's involvement in the municipal council elections. Attar said; "We demanded that women hold at least three seats in their local municipal council. Even if a woman did not win she still has a right to participate in the work of the council."

The women in the Jeddah Chamber of Commerce and Industry continue to offer women financial and legal services. OlfetQabbani, former chairwoman of the chamber's Industrial Committee, called for the transformation of women from administrators to productive industrialists and the provision of incentives to industrialists who employ women. The chamber has been able to offer substantial support to many women in business and has provided them opportunities to conduct business with international companies.

The Jeddah Chamber of Commerce encourages women to explore new business opportunities across the globe. It organizes business trips for Saudi business women and includes successful business women in trade delegations. Their presence always adds to the success of the missions.

The chamber also introduces business women to visiting trade delegations and encourages their participation to foster better trade relations.

Earlier the Khadija Bint Khuwailed Business Center for Women succeeded in its relentless efforts to make the Ministry of Commerce scrap the "legal representative" condition for women to conduct their businesses. The business center is a major driving force lobbying for new laws and regulations to support working women as well as protecting the interests of women in the business community.

Social activist and economist Alia Banaja, who is calling for the abolition of the "legal guardian" system, led another ongoing campaign. Her campaign is aimed at all ministries and government departments that insist women need to have a male guardian to run their lives. In an open letter to the Ministry of Labor the campaigners rejected the definition of the guardianship rule and stressed that society could no longer accept the treatment of women as minors and urged the ministry to apply justice for all. Banaja noted that, "They are backward in realizing the needs of the age, and they are stuck to certain out-dated sets of conditions and beliefs."

Meanwhile, ReemAsaad, economic writer, member of the Saudi Economic association, and women's rights advocate, led a successful campaign to boycott lingerie stores managed by salesmen. She began her campaign in 2008 and criticized the Ministry of Labor for not implementing the decision to replace the salesmen with women, which was issued in 2005 but was never implemented. Asaad also called for hiring saleswomen in management, accounting and customer service as a step towards enabling women to enter economic and professional domains.

Fatima Qarub, headed the campaign titled, "Enough with Embarrassment", confirming that many women experienced embarrassing situations with salesmen in lingerie stores. The Saudi women's revolutionary Facebook campaign, chaired by NohaAlsolaiman, was also among the most popular and effective ones. These campaigns and others continue to put pressure for change and demand for the right to live with honour and dignity.

The campaigns succeeded in getting the attention of government officials after thousands joined the calls on Facebook and Twitter.

Ultimately King Abdullah ordered the immediate employment of women in lingerie stores and fining anyone who violated the order. More than 28,000 women initially applied for the jobs and the Ministry of Labor established a hotline to receive calls on any abuse or violation against the rule to facilitate a safe and comfortable environment for the saleswomen. The ministry even provided training for the new employees.

Dr.SamiaAlamoudi an associate Professor at King Abdul Aziz University and a consultant Obstetrician Gynacologist, lead a successful breast awareness campaign. She is recognized for her courageous campaign to raise awareness about the prevalence of breast cancer in Saudi Arabia and for her bold initiative to speak about her own experience as a breast cancer survivor to show support for other women who suffer in silence Her story has been included in the secondary schools English curriculum since 2008 , "People who made a difference." Her dedicated and pioneer campaign to raise awareness about the disease in her country and community won her many national and international awards.

Dr. Al Amoudi, has received several awards for her efforts. She has been nominated by Arabian Business Magazine to be among the top 100 who have had an impact on their societies, and she was also listed as one of the most influential Arab scientists.

Princess Reema Bandar Bin Sultan also campaigned to raise awareness about breast cancer in Saudi Arabia. She led a group of 10 brave and physically fit young women to climb to a base camp on Mount Everest. Her successful campaign made headline news and was the pride of the nation. Her team women were nick named by the local media "the Pink Warriors" and the initiative had a very positive impact at home and abroad.

Such campaigns are needed to increase pressure for change and demand the right of every woman to be respected and live in dignity. These bold initiatives are essential to pave the way towards a better future for the next generation. The wisdom and dedication of women in leadership positions can help Saudi Arabia build a stronger more-cultured society and project a more respected image of Saudi women to the rest of the world.

Cultural Contributions of Prominent Women

Barakat Trust

HamidaAlireza is a prominent Saudi woman who has made significant cultural contributions. She has dedicated much of her time to preserve Islamic Art and Saudi ethnic designs and costumes. She is a trustee, board member and co-founder of Barakat Foundation as well as founder and active member of Almansujat Foundation.

The Barakat Trust foundation is a UK registered charity that provides financial support for the study and research of the material and visual culture of Islamic Art. It provides scholarships and grants in Islamic art history, architecture and archaeology in reputable academic institutions at post graduate and post-doctoral level. It also supports archeological excavations and surveys to enrich and preserve Islamic art. The foundation sponsors projects that present useful contributions to the knowledge and history of Islamic art and archeology, and it promotes and distributes Islamic art and literature.

The trust also supports exhibitions, lectures, conferences to enhance cross-cultural understanding and tolerance.Her mission is also to encourage Saudis and other Arabs to pursue this path of preserving the Muslim heritage and becoming experts in the field, which has been dominated so far by non-Arabs and non-Muslims.

Mansujat Foundation

Hamida and her sister Nadya with other members of the family and friends founded"Mansujat"another non-profit foundation with a mission to revive and preserve the traditional and ethnic designs and costumes of various regions of Saudi Arabia. The foundation conducts research from the cultural history of the region to raise awareness and build national and international appreciation of this unique heritage. So far the foundation has exhibited the authentic and unique costume collection at the British Museum and various events in Paris, the United States and Singapore and plans to exhibit their valuable collection around the world.

The Saudi Art Movement

Saudi artists are gaining recognition in the regional and global contemporary art scene. They continue to hold regular exhibitions and participate in international art fairs projecting a more positive image of Saudi Arabia in the international arena. Saudi media has covered many success stories of prominent Saudi contemporary artists who have exhibited their work in local and international Museums and Galleries. Saudi artist Manal Al Dowayan is one of the most prominent among the new wave artists. She interacts with the public through talks and art projects. Her latest contribution is on the concept of "free-zones" at Art Dubai Global Forum, a platform allowing writers, artists and researchers to engage in dialogues on the most interesting and crucial topics.

Princess ReemAlfaisalis a prominent Saudi photographer who elo-quently defines herself as a Muslim artist sprung from native Saudi culture and history, "In my art I am seeking to show signs of the Divine in na-ture and in man. For me, light is one of the many manifestations of God, which He casts in our path through life to remind us of His constant pres-ence in ourselves and in every place. Every photograph is a pattern of light and shade. For me, my photography is a way to praise God's glory in the universe."Both women have truly exhibited art, culture and class — ideal images we should develop within our society.

There is a need to instil the love of art and style in our children and build their artistic talent. More should be done to promote the culture of art on a national scale, and it should be included in the school curriculum. The public must learn to appreciate beauty and recognize works of art. The young should be acquainted with the artistic contributions of the Saudi pioneers of the art movement from the early '70s to the present day. Foremost among them is Safia Bin Zagr who studied fine arts and graphics at St. Martin's College of Arts in London and has won many national and international awards. She should be recognized for her dedication to record the history of the Saudi *Hijazi* cultural heritage, its customs and traditions. In 1979, she published her first book, "Saudi Arabia: An Artist's Point of View of the Past." It was translated in English and French. Bin Zagr continued to hold exhibitions in the Kingdom and abroad. In 1997 she founded her own museum The *DaratSafiyaBinzagr* which includes a library of art and literary works and a studio to provide courses in drawing and painting. BinZagr launched a website featuring her work globally. Bin Zagr holds yearly public events to promote the arts culture in Saudi society, and she holds a monthly cultural and educational gathering in her own residence to inspire intellectual dialogue and create social awareness among Saudi women.

Princess Jawahir Bint Majid a genuine patron of Art, heads the non-profit AlmansouriaArt Foundation to support and encourage Saudi artists and promote the culture of art among Saudi citizens. She has been instrumental in nurturing Saudi and Middle Eastern artists and revealed the art and culture of Saudi Arabia to the rest of the world. She was nominated among the 50 most influential cultural players in the world for her contributions to the region's art scene.

The foundation has published a series of impressive art books and strives to project the work of the talented Saudi artists. Ithas supported many Saudis to adopt the universal language of art to reach out to other cultures and share common ground within the global contemporary movement. Among them is Dia Aziz Dia, a prominent Saudi artist who projects his daily environment in his art. Dia, who trained as a sculptor in Italy, is the designer and creator on many public monuments in materials ranging from marble to concrete and bronze. He has been awarded numerous awards and has gained international recognition, exhibiting his works in many art exhibitions.

Almansouria also established in Paris theArt Studio that plays an active role in promoting new forms of art. The Art Studio provides the opportunity to many Saudi artists to exhibit their work in Paris and communicate with the French public and exchange views with the most prominent French artists.

Mona Khizindar has been recognized as a global figure and professional curator of contemporary art and photography. She became the first Saudi woman to be appointed Director General of the "Institute du Monde Arabe," (IMA) in 2012. For many years Khizindar was responsible for the IMA's permanent collection, which exercised great influence on the international cultural scene. The Forum of Arab Women also elected her as the Woman of the Year. Khizindarsays that women play a central role in the evolution of society.

King Abdullah's reforms,which include promoting art and culture, continue despite the confrontation between tradition and modernity. Saudi Artists have shown great determination to pursue the reform path that King Abdullah initiated. In the course of eight years the reform movement has been geared towards keeping the society competitive in a very competitive world. Reformers are striving to muzzle the obstructionists and replace pointless, deviant misguidance with wonderful opportunities for the young men and women in this country. There should be more concerted efforts to promote the culture of art and revive the beauty of Islamic art in order to help Saudi Arabia modernize. Corporations abroad support and encourage budding artists who cannot afford the expenses of exhibiting their work. Saudi corporations need to show more support towards Saudi artists and invest in young talent to promote the culture of art in the Kingdom. The success of the Saudi artists' movement will create a better world for the younger generation.

Prominent Philanthropists

Princess Sara Alfaisal and Princess ModiBintKhaled are the founders of Al-Nahda Philanthropic Society. The society is the first and most successful charity organization in Saudi Arabia today. It was founded in 1962 by Princess Sara Alfaisal and a group of dedicated volunteers to provide charity work in Riyadh. Princess Sara is the chairman of the society, and Princess ModiBintKhaled is the secretary general. The charitable society has initiated several projects to empower women and support the underprivileged. Itcontinues to support the poor and needy women and offers training and literacy programs to empower womensocially and economically.

One of its successes is the "My Heritage" project,which helps women master the skills of traditional handicrafts of Saudi Arabia. The society provides women from all regions with funding and logistical support to market their products across the Kingdom.

The society has also signed a preliminary memorandum of understanding with King Saud UniversityCenter forHumanitarian Colleges to encourage voluntary work within the community.

The team of highly qualified women working and volunteering in Al-Nahda society have played a great role in creating a positive change in society. A large number of girls have benefitted from the various educational programs offered, and they have been inspired to continue their education and learn skills to become contributing members of society.

SuadJaffali is an active philanthropist who donates generously to many academic institutions at home and abroad. She founded the first women's welfare society in Jeddah and established the Help Center, a remarkable special-education institution for mentally handicapped children. Jaffali established the Ahmed and SuadJaffaliEndowment Scholarship Fund in 1985, and she is the managing director of Ahmed JaffaliBenevolent Foundation. She is a board member of the Arab Thought Foundation and Dar Al Hekma University and also the overseas board of the Lebanese American University. The prominent philanthropist is an active member of the board of trustees at the International Academy in Amman, a member of the Institute of Palestinian Studies in Washington,D.C., and supports Dar Al TiflAlarabiOrphanage in Jerusalem.

Sultana Ali Reza is founder and chief executive director of the Jeddah Institute for Speech and Hearing (JISH), a non-profit institution that provides speech, language and hearing services to improve the wellbeing of patients with hearing impairment. JISH is the only center of its kind in the Kingdom. Ali Reza devoted her life to her three children with hearing impairment and decided to establish JISH in 1991 to provide a service that was not available elsewhere in the Kingdom. The center has cared for many patients and has provided a much-needed service to both patients and families who needed guidance to care for family members with special needs.

Ali Reza established a scholarship program with San Jose State University to train Saudi and Arab speech pathologists, audiologists and therapists. Four Saudi women have succeeded, and they now hold masters' degrees in speech pathology and audiology. Her dedication and personal interest in providing global standards and quality care for her patients is the reason behind the popularity and success of the center.

Saudi Women Writers Influence Change

The state of chaos and turmoil in Egypt and the conflicts and wars in many Arab and Muslim countries today are quite alarming. The dangers and instabilities that are so close to home should put us all on high alert and fill us with determination to protect our homeland and address our challenges with transparency and sincerity to guarantee social stability and justice for all.

We live in an age in which information is available at the click of a button. Censorship and secrecy are things of the past; they have become obsolete thanks to Twitter and YouTube. Governments can no longer apply censorship policies or lie to their people. The younger generation is well informed and continues to demand better opportunities and services that are available in other societies around them. Citizens today demand greater participation and wish to have a say in laws and policies that affect their lives. This makes it imperative to have a free press and professional writers and journalists who can be the voices of the people and be a bridge between the public and the government in order to avoid strife and create a stable and peaceful society.

In Saudi Arabia the role of media is more crucial because it has a responsibility to influence the mindset of a very closed community. Experts in the field have a duty to change the cultural barriers detrimental to progress. Writers and journalists must strive to educate the public on vital matters that impact their lives. They should identify malfeasance and injustice and bring them to the attention of the authorities in order to find solutions to develop a more stable and harmonious society.

Women represent 50 percent of Saudi society. When women are granted their legal rights and are empowered to serve their community our society will prosper and our families will thrive. In 2006, Dr.Hatoon Al-Fassi, the activist, academic and bold weekly columnist at Al-Riyadh newspaper, initiated the Saudi Women Writers'Online Network to address civil reform issues and women's rights in Saudi Arabia. Dr. Al-Fassi, who is a well-known historian and has lectured as an assistant professor of women's history at King Saud University, continues to energize this exclusive writers' network with strong articles that address the legal rights of women in Saudi Arabia.

Similarly, this group of prolific women writers has contributed with constructive articles to guarantee the welfare of women, many of whom remain unaware of their basic human rights. Within a period of six years, the group grew to include 70 members — talented writers and columnists ofboth Arabic and English newspapers. The group includes Aziza Al-Manie, Thuraya Oraid, Fatina Shaker, Fawzia Abu Khaled, Fawzia Al-Bakr, Samar Al-Miqrin, Nabila Mahjoub, Reem Asaad, Amira Kashghari, Halimah Muzafar, Fatin Bundugji, Maram Makawi, Badria Albishr, Suhaila ZainAlabdin and many others who are recognized by both the public and the authorities as responsible advocates for change. The group also includes honorary members who have contributed to society such as Dr.ThorayaObaid, former executive director of the United Nations and newly-appointed member of the Shoura Council, and Dr.Thuraya Al-Turki, a well-known anthropologist.

These women are the voice of the people and a powerful force in building the nation. They have been instrumental in changing the mindset of people and educating those who are influenced by rigid customs that stand in the way of empowering women and creating a harmonious environment for the modern Saudi family.

Many Saudi women suffer in silence not knowing who to turn to or what legal procedures are available for help. Saudi women writers have become a source of strength, protecting the underprivileged and the oppressed and projecting their sufferings by addressing many cases of abuse when legal channels fail, such as the "Qatif rape case," the divorce of Fatma and Mansour, cases of domestic violence and child marriages.

Among their great achievements is thecampaign to include women in the decision making process. Dr. Al-Fassi,Naila Attar and other members of the group initiated the *Baladi* Campaign, which called for women's participation in municipal elections. Today women have become members of the Shoura Council, and they will participate in the 2015 municipal council elections. The writers' network also continues to campaign against the guardianship rule and the elimination of other discriminatory rules marginalizing the role of women in society.

The bold and eloquent women writers have had an impact, and their contributions cannot be ignored. They represent the public opinions of the educated citizens of this country who are eager to contribute to the welfare of society.

The Women Writers' Online Network is focused on highlighting the challenges of modern society. The group offers analysis to help the public form opinions and make judgments regarding various controversial issues. They strive to keep the public informed about what is happening in society. They work collectively to affect people's perspectives through their progressive and objective analysis of matters that influence our daily lives. Their critique and differing opinions should not be viewed by the authorities as dissent but rather as support to build a strong nation.

Media awareness campaigns are necessary to educate the public about their rights and responsibilities to their country. Citizens should learn to respect the rule of law, and the government should protect the interests of its citizens. That is why the role of the media is crucial in protecting our society from chaos and distress.

Officials should promote media independence and freedom to allow responsible journalists and columnists to voice the needs and concerns of the people. The stability and progress of the nation will be ensured when the media is supported so that it can act as a watchdog for change and reform.

Women in Sports

The decision to ban aberrant edicts or *fatwas* has created a sense of optimism and renewed confidence in government initiatives to combat extremist ideology. These *fatwas* were spoiling the lives of the people and making them miserable in their own country. It is sad how Saudis had to count the days between vacations in order to travel and enjoy freedom and joy in another land.

One of the most harmful *fatwas* and a source of public discontent was one declaring physical exercise and sports for girls immoral and un-Islamic. The *fatwa* claimed that it would be un-Islamic because girls would be imitating boys and acquiring masculine attitudes. Based on this *fatwa* physical education was banned in girls' public schools, and women were not legally allowed to take part in sports anywhere in the Kingdom.

LinaAlmaeena has been calling for the rights of women to exercise since 2006. A strong sports advocate, she was determined to influence change and campaigned to introduce basketball for girls in Jeddah. She appeared on talk shows, radio and television and wrote articles about the need to promote a healthier lifestyle for women, so as to protect them from many maladies caused by the lack of exercise. She was very effective and was encouraged by society and officials to raise awareness about the right of every woman and child to stay fit and healthy by exercising and playing sports.

Almaeena is the founder and team captain of Jeddah United, a local sports company in Jeddah. After three years of campaigning she established her sports company in 2006, and until today she and her husband (who heads the sports division for boys) continue to organize sports events for young girls and boys to build Saudi athletes and prepare them to compete in national and international events. She has debated many prominent religious scholars who advocated the ban on physical exercise in girls' schools. Her relentless campaign encouraged sports culture among the young and projected a positive attitude toward women's sports within the society. Eventually in 2012 the Ministry of Education officially recognized the need to introduce physical education in girls schools and later announced that soon it will be building new girls schools with indoor sports facilities across the Kingdom.

Hopefully this move will be followed by the elimination of other strict rules that are imposed in the name of Islam and allow for more flexible attitudes that promote emotional and physical wellbeing in young people's lives.

Almaeena's determination and continuous activities to promote the culture of physical wellness makes her one of the most prominent young Saudi women who has influenced change and progress in Saudi Arabia.

She has crowned her efforts to promote physical exercise for Saudi women by joining a group of 10 women to climb to the first camp of Mount Everest in 2012.

The Culture of Sports and the OlympicsMovement

Saudi Arabia celebrated the success of the Saudi Olympic Equestrian Team, which won the bronze medal at the 2012 Olympics in London. This was the first team medal for Saudi Arabia. The four team members, Kamal Bahamdan, Prince Abdullah Al-Saud, Ramzi Al-Duhami and Abdullah Sharbatly, are heroes who have boosted Saudi public morale.

However the Saudi female athletes Wojdan Shahrkhani and Sarah Attar who made sports history for Saudi women were completely ignored. Wojdan who competed in the +78kg judo heavyweight category, and Sarah in the 800-meter event were the first Saudi women ever to compete in the Olympics. They represent the younger generation of women who are competitive and will not give up their right to exercise and lead a healthy lifestyle. They should have been given a heroes' welcome upon their return.

It is unfortunate that their participation in the Olympics triggered a strong online attack by some ultraconservatives who slandered them and denounced their initiative as un-Islamic. However, it was very rewarding to witness the prompt response from even louder voices of sports enthusiasts who congratulated them and supported their determination to compete in the global event. LinaAlmaeena, a long time campaigner for sports for women in Saudi Arabia, was proud of their historic participation in the Olympic games, and she is already making plans to qualify her Jeddah United Basketball team for the 2016 Olympics in Rio de Janeiro.

The Saudi government in 2012 was finally pressured to take a firm stand against the ultra-conservatives. It had been under intense pressure from the International Olympic Committee and human-rights groups to include female athletes. After months of IOC negotiations with Saudi Arabia to include women in the Olympic Games, the government finally put a stop to one of the *fatwas* that declared physical exercise and sports for girls immoral and un-Islamic. Such *fatwas* and restrictions now belong to the past. The Kingdom is witnessing a new era in which women have been granted official approval to participate in the Olympics; the government has allocated a large budget to build sports facilities in girls' schools and the Ministry of Education has announced that it will include physical exercise in the school curriculum.

Meanwhile, more needs to be done to promote the culture of sports and to encourage young Saudis to become better athletes. There is no substitute for proper training and serious exercise. Young athletes need to understand the value of discipline and hard work in order to qualify for the next Olympic Games. What is also needed is a better strategy to identify and train young talented athletes and to Olympic standards.

It is equally important to promote the culture of the Olympics Movement and its universal values of excellence, friendship and respect. These values are the foundation upon which the Olympics Movement combines sports, culture and education for the betterment of humankind.

The value of excellence is based on giving one's best; it is not only about winning, but also about participating, achieving personal goals and striving to do one's best with a strong mind and body. Aspiring men and women athletes need to know that the Olympic Movement is also about friendship and building a better world through sports. It provides a model for effort, dedication and creates commonality for people of more than 200 countries despite political, economic, gender, racial or religious differences. It provides financial and the programmed support for the development of athletes and the advancement of women in the world of sports. These core values are brought to life through the principles of humanism, universality and the alliance between sports, education and culture.

Many Saudis watched the Olympics daily and followed the progress of their team. Media professionals should always take this opportunity to stress the Olympic principle that the practice of sports is a human right, and that every individual must have the opportunity to participate.

There is a growing sense of optimism spreading among sports advocates and enthusiasts throughout the Kingdom. Saudi athletes are the pride of the nation and the hope for a better future. They have the backing of a vibrant, young generation eager to see them succeed and compete for gold medals. Educators and media professionals have an obligation to support our athletes and project the universal character of the Olympic Movement, its respected global presence and its distinctive success. Above all, the Saudi public needs to be aware that Olympic values matter to all peace-loving citizens of our modern world.

A Story of Dreams and Aspirations

Princess Reema Bint Bandar Bin Sultan Al-Saud, the founding member of the Zahra Breast Cancer Association, assembled a team of 10 women who shared the same passion in spreading the message on breast cancer awareness to every corner of the country. The all-woman team was determined to share their difficult journey with breast cancer victims who often suffer in silence, hopeful that all those women would gain a little bit of optimism and inspiration from the team's own struggles on Mt. Everest.

The mission was of endurance and perseverance through some very harsh and dangerous conditions. Perhaps what made it more exceptional was that it was being undertaken by Saudi women, long portrayed as a marginalized segment of Saudi society. They went through extensive training for six months to prepare themselves for their biggest challenge.

Hasna'a Mokhtar, a public relations manager and one of the climbers, recounts how she prepared herself with intensive physical training. "My training helped me somewhat in dealing with the steep, winding paths and uneven terrain. It was also a struggle to move because of the biting cold and the high altitude. We were told to concentrate on taking only one step at a time and not to look too far ahead because it would only highlight the enormity of the task and would end up frustrating or demotivating us."

Raha Moharrak, an art director, said their main struggle was coping with the harsh environment and being unable to wash or change their clothes or be in touch with the outside world. "We would climb for eight hours nonstop and then sleep in shelters that did not keep the cold away. We would shiver all night in our sleeping bags." Raised in a warm desert environment, one can only imagine how cold it must have been for the climbers.

As they reached 15,000 feet, the group faced incredible physical challenges. Shortness of breath, nausea and headaches were their constant companions as they silently trod upwards. One climber, Hatun Madani, a real estate agent, sprained her ankle; another, Samaher Mously, a business analyst, developed blisters on her feet that would not stop bleeding. Hasna'a's knees began acting up, while LinaAlmaeena was enveloped in light-headed nausea. On the way up they met other trekkers who told them to go back because some had lost their lives, but one and all, they were determined to succeed.

After eight days of hardship, the 11 Saudi women finally reached their goal.

LinaAlmaeena, the sports advocate, said she would do it again and again to raise more awareness. RahaMoharrak and Mona Shahab, a child clinical psychologist, are already making plans to conquer Europe's highest peak, Mount Elbrus (5,642 m/ 18,510 ft) in the Caucasus Mountains for any worthwhile social cause.

They started on their journey as near strangers, and they returned as sisters.

Mashael Alhejelan, a pulmonary and critical-care consultant physician; AsmaAlghaleb, a journalist;Alya Al-Saad, a water entertainment activity business owner; and Nora Bouzo, publisher of Oasis magazine; all agreed that their victory formed an everlasting sweet memory and stimulated their appetite for further challenges for good causes. Kudos to the brave Saudi women, for they have raised the bar so high that young women and men will find it difficult to quit when they encounter problems or hardships. The adventures of these young women — conquering heights for a noble cause — is the sort of bedtime story that should be popularized among young girls for years to come.

A Ministry for Women's Affairs

Conferences, forums and symposiums aplenty have been held in Saudi Arabia calling for the empowerment of women and raising public awareness about women's valuable contributions towards a more advanced society at par with the rest of the world.

Perhaps the most significant Forum was held in Dec. 2011 entitled "Participation of Women in National Development" where women called for the establishment of a Ministry for Women's Affairs.

Many women still believe that a ministry directed to implement a national strategy to support the empowerment of women in Saudi Arabia would assure that progress continues without any cultural, economic or political impediments. Such a ministry would be ideal to implement equal treatment policies and maximize women's contributions toward a more prosperous future.

Saudi women need a positive force to dispel misconceptions that lead to negative attitudes. Such a ministry could be a credible power in society to propose measures to counter current discriminatory practices against women.

There is no shortage of research and case studies of women facing hardship and social injustice, but there also is no governmental body directly charged to do anything with the findings. According to Saudi social scientists, the reasons behind the exploitation of women by husbands and guardians within our society are mainly the absence of deterrent laws or the failure to implement existing laws. Therefore, such a ministry could develop policies and directives to address the rights of women and find remedies for those who suffer in silence, the abused and the underprivileged.

If new civil or commercial codes have to be created to empower women, such a ministry also could serve as the women's advocate during governmental deliberations on the amendment of current codes.

There are many women's issues requiring both a governmental and a societal change, including unemployment, domestic abuse, sexual harassment, emotional blackmail and that pervasive attitude of disrespect. A Ministry for Women's Affairs would be an appropriate champion of women's legal rights and an authority to outline their duties and responsibilities as citizens.

The integration of women into the workforce is key to the nation's progress and development. The ministry of women's affairs could eliminate the barriers that exist in the labor market. Many issues need to be addressed including wage parity, and perhaps pension reforms. Hopefully it would work hand-in-hand with the business community and current regulatory bodies so that needed reforms are understood, accepted and put into play.

Another important objective for our society should be to include women in all ministries, government departments and organizations. There are many women with great capabilities and impressive credentials who would qualify for ministerial posts and leadership positions. It would not be difficult to identify women capable of running a Ministry for Women's Affairs.

Leading business women assert that such a ministry could put in place policies on public matters, civil and business affairs that would finally address their needs. It would demonstrate the political will to empower women as equal citizens, so they can better contribute to the security, prosperity and advancement of the country.

Strengthening the image of Saudi women in the international community is another area that needs work. It is unfortunate that the rigid position of many women in this country has harmed the image of all the Muslim women worldwide. It also has compromised the role of Saudi Arabia as the leader of the Muslim world. Saudi women can play a more positive, political role that can project Arab and Islamic issues on the world stage. Therefore, a ministry for women could establish a strong and reliable entity to reach out to women leaders in other countries and international women organizations in order to bridge the gap between Saudi women and the international community.

The global marketplace is evolving rapidly, and Saudi Arabia cannot afford to effectively sideline half its population any longer without dire consequences to the nation's prosperity. A Ministry for Women's Affairs could ensure that progress is orderly and in step with our faith and culture and that it happens instead of remaining a discussion point for years to come.

Chapter 5

SAUDI YOUTH AND FAMILY CHALLENGES

- Youth Empowerment
- Youth Participation
- Youth Forums
- Youth Diplomacy
- Saudi Chinese Youth Forum
- Saudi Brazilian Youth Program
- Saudi Youth outline their experience in Germany
- Saudi Indian youth forum
- Saudi Korean Visit
- Modern Society and the Traditional Family

Youth Empowerment

Young Saudis of the 21st Century are more exposed to other cultures and more aware of worlddevelopments than at any other time in the Kingdom's history. Thanks to the influx of digital media and the devices that support it they have immediate access to information. They do not need to be spoon fed knowledge. At the click of a button they receive the latest information and are updated with the political developments around the globe. They are empowered by the social media and inspired by the youth in neighboring countries that have overcome the fear factor and demand to have their voices heard, rejecting the status quo of corruption and self-serving agendas.

An old patriarchal system that does not address the needs of the young will not find any support from them

In the Saudi Arabia of today, the government is beginning to recognize the immense potential of the young and has set up programs to build their professional and vocational skills.

The country buzzes with youth activities, and there is a sense of urgency to address the needs of young men and women and create better opportunities for them to participate in nation building

Youth Participation

The Shoura Council's Social, Family and Youth Affairs Committee adopted a recommendation to restructure the Presidency of Youth Welfare and turn it into a ministry. The recommendation was based on the Presidency's 2010 and 2011annual reports, however it is very unfortunate that the Council voted against it.

According to the 2012 official statisticsthe Saudi population breaks down as follows:

- 0-14 years: 29.4% (male 3,939,377/female 3,754,020)
- 15-64 years:67.6% (male 9,980,253/female 7,685,328)
- 65 years and over:3% (male 404,269/female368,456) (2011 est.)

A Ministry of Youth Affairs could elevate the importance of youth-related issues in the Council of Ministers and other state sectors. This would guarantee a more effective contribution by the young peoplewho are the future leaders and an essential factor in the country's economic and social development. The future of the country depends on them, and giving an opportunity could lead the nation to greater heights.

The reform movement in Saudi Arabia has given the younger generation greater attention, and national budgets have been geared to education and the development of youth-related affairs. However, it is important to assess the development of these programs in order to ensure that they are on the right track. Perhaps strategies should be revised for maximum effect. Better policies should be implemented to advance the most valuable human resource of the country, and better incentives should be provided to empower our future leaders. Their success or failure could influence the direction of our nation.

Building a Knowledge-Based Society

The government is under pressure to accelerate educational reforms and upgrade the educational system with more capable teaching faculties to establishworld-classtechnical universities. The objective is to produce knowledgeable and competent graduates,capable of addressing the needs of a Saudi society that wants and needs to take its place in an increasingly complex and competitive technology-driven world.

Saudi economistDr.Abdul Aziz Aljazzar during the 2010 US-Saudi Business Opportunities Forum in Chicagohighlighted the process of building a knowledge-based society. He outlined some of Saudi Arabia's achievements in the information and communication technology (ICT) sector, which included an Internet penetration of nearly 30 percent and a fiber-optics infrastructure already in place. Information technology has become a focal point of the education system; this is demonstrated by the Kingdom's Ninth Five-Year Development Plan, which emphasizes the importance of creating a knowledge-based economy and is supported by a \$3 billion (SR11.25 billion) investment in e-government programs.

There have been many mistakes in the past, and some government officials have failed to provide quality services to help our young people realize their full potential. The state remains responsibleforenforcing necessary laws that can ensure the safety and wellbeing of our young people.

It is time to involve our youth in research related to their needs and challenges, and use their input to develop policies that ensure their rights. Our young people can provide accurate information that will allow decision makers to formulate more effective youth-related policies, laws and regulations. A youth ministry could engage young people and provide them the opportunity to come up with innovative ideas and offer solutions for their problems. It would become the ideal ministry for implementing the necessary measures to alleviate poverty, provide a healthy environment, develop community awareness, organize and encourage public activities and events as well as to initiate and monitor international youth exchange programs. A youth ministry would be more reliable in monitoring and taking the responsibility for managing all youth affairs. Perhaps including a youth committee in the Shoura Council could also be a more effective means to address the needs of our large and expanding youth population.

Either or both of these propositions would allow our young to share in the decision-making process. Such an initiative would promote national solidarity and influence change. It would enhance the sense of patriotism among our youth and encourage their participation in the building of the nation. Engaging our young people and encouraging their participation through a ministry that they could relate to and connect with may be the ideal solution to their problems and frustrations. It would give young people a voice and allow them to communicate their ideas. It would motivate them to produce and strive to make their dreams come true.

Youth volunteerism needs to be further nurtured and promoted. Our youth demonstrated its willingness and proved their capabilities in volunteer work during the devastating Jeddah floodsof December 2010. We need to capitalize on this new movement that has given our young people a sense of pride and inner satisfaction. A Ministry ofYouth Affairs could support community service programs. Training the young to serve their community through organized volunteer work could help create a more stable and harmonious society.

A youth ministry could also develop youth diplomacy and promote international youth exchange. It would be effective in initiating intercultural dialogue between Saudi youth and the rest of the world. Encouraging global exchange would give our young people a sense of pride and allow them to explain their culture and traditions to their counterparts around the world and it would give them an opportunity to assert their role within the global community.

The Presidency of Youth Welfare has been ineffective and has not catered to the needs of the young in spite of the millions that have been spent to support our athletes and encourage a sports culture in society.

Our youth dream of qualifying for the Olympics; they aspire to win medals and gain international recognition. We must not continue to fail them. A Ministry of Youth Affairs could be more effective with a stronger capacity for coordinating on an official level. The development of the sports sector must be given greater priority. A ministry would be in a better position to formulate effective strategies with meaningful funds and human resources to achieve the aspirations of our young befitting the country's reputation and position.

A Ministry of Youth Affairs would be the ideal solution for protecting the rights of our young people and promoting their interests and wellbeing. Domestic violence, broken homes, crime and drug addiction are on the rise. Social scientists stress the need to address psychological and economic needs to protect the youth from stressful conditions that lead them astray and put them in harm's way. Researchers constantly voice their concerns over inappropriate services. It is time we implemented well-researched strategies that can be more effective in eradicating poverty and in providing job opportunities, better wages and more decent housing conditions in order to build a healthy, productive generation. The rights of our young people should be respected. There is an urgency to enforce laws to protect them and create policies to address their needs.

Youth Forums

Youth forums have attracted the support of government, academic institutions, businesses and NGOs across the Kingdom.

Internet forums continue to embolden young men and women to confront their problems and come up with positive solutions. The cyber community has certainly empowered the younger generation and has energized them to play a larger role in society.

These forums have helped address the needs of young people and bridge the generation gap. The government has begun to recognize that today's young men and women are a different generation; they are more exposed to the world and have access to the latest research and developments across the globe. They are the "Facebook generation," and they interact with one another and share both their ideas and frustrations. They have gained strength and unity through Internet forums that have given them the courage to speak up and create a voice that demands to be heard.

Youth forums are gaining popularity with young people calling for swifter action to eliminate obstacles to much-needed reforms, such as upgrading the educational system, more job opportunities, effective training programs, small business opportunities, better treatment in government departments and more entertainment facilities. They are legitimate demands that would guarantee young men and women a life of dignity and prosperity at par with the more advanced societies of the world. These forums also have energized young men and women by directing attention to their concerns and creating initiatives catering to their needs.

One of the most impressive forums was initiated by Effat University during the 2011 Jeddah Economic Forum. The university organized an event in which 2,000 young men and women were invited to rank the most effective youth initiatives during Jeddah's disastrous two floods. They shared their stories demonstrating how Facebook, Twitter, i-Phone and Blackberry communications got assistance to flood victims in record time, saved many lives and efficiently distributed aid to many remote and isolated parts of the city.

The open and transparent dialogue between young people and Makkah Governor Prince Khaled Al-Faisal was another inspiring event that came at the conclusion of the forum. More than 1,500 young men and women provided a glimpse into the mindset of the young as they highlighted their aspirations and frustrations.

The halls were filled with young people who actively took part in the transparent, bold discussions. Young women boldly asked when will they be permitted to drive, and young men called for more rights such as a seat in the Shoura Council. During the meeting, the governor promised the establishment of cultural, social and sports clubs for both men and women and a monthly meeting with young men and women that would enable them to express their viewpoints on issues that concern their future and allow them to submit proposals to address their needs and aspirations.

The announcements were very encouraging and boosted the morale of the young audience inspiring them to freely share their concerns with their governor.

The National Dialogue Center has conducted several sessions across the country to address crucial issues such as unemployment, education, tribalism and extremism. The young men and women involved demonstrated great talent and potential as they discussed the issues intelligently and called for better opportunities and improved government services to improve the standard of living for the young.

The youth forums also have strengthened the resolve among young women across the Kingdom to speak out against bias and narrow-mindedness and overcome their frustrations with positive initiatives to serve society and achieve a more prosperous future. Young women, who represent perhaps 30 percent of society today, refuse to be marginalized. They have become more vocal in academic forums and used social media to expose negative attitudes that stand in the way of social progress and economic development. They stress the need for a holistic interpretation of Islamic principles that recognize the rights of women in the 21st century.

The youth forums are certainly having a great impact on society with a new drive to influence change and development. Therefore, it is important that the government, academic institutions, businesses and NGOs continue to support youth forums that encourage youth participation and also provide an excellent opportunity to identify potential leaders who can lead the nation to greater prosperity.

Youth Diplomacy

The Ministry of Foreign Affairs initiated international youth forums to build bridges of understanding between Saudi youth and the rest of the world. The success of the first such initiative, "The Saudi-British Youth Forum" held in the UK in 2009 paved the way for other. more successful youth forums in other countries. The Saudi British Forum included young men and women fromboth Britain and Saudi Arabia who met to discuss issues of mutual concern and to learn more about each other. Moreover, they shared experiences and proposed some joint projects between Saudi and British organizations to encourage better business opportunities between the youth of the two Kingdoms.

The Saudi and British youth were inspired by the speeches of their foreign ministers during the closing session of the fourth meeting of the Two Kingdoms Dialogue that was held in Riyadh on April 8, 2009. They outlined their recommendations on building trust and understanding between the two nations and called for greater participation of youth in the decision-making process.

Foreign Minister Prince Saud Al-Faisal, addressing the leaders of the both nations' business communities and their future leaders, commended the achievements of the Youth Forum and praised continuing meetings between the young people, which have provided them with excellent opportunities to get better acquainted with one another and to better understand varied views of the future.

British Foreign Secretary David Miliband praised the dialogue that has helped greatly to improve bilateral ties between Saudi Arabia and the United Kingdom. He said the two countries should work together to build a global society more conducive to dialogue, tolerance and moderation.

The Saudi and British officials reviewed the great successes of the two Youth Forums in fostering better relations between the two countries. The first forum was held in Britain in November 2007; the second was initiated with the objective of boosting cultural dialogue and partnership through pilot projects designed by youth organizations from both countries.

The Second Saudi-British Youth Forum was held in January 2011 in Jeddah and Riyadh with 48 young participants from the UK and Saudi Arabia. The Committee of International Trade (CIT) in the Council of Saudi Chambers of Commerce and Industry organized and funded the seven-day event in cooperation with the British Youth Council and under the patronage of the Saudi Ministry of Foreign Affairs.

A documentary filmreviewed the events of the two youth forums and presented an impressive account of the joint venture, which began in Jeddah where the young participants attended workshops at the Jeddah Chamber of Commerce and Industry to identify common values and goals. They planned joint projects that could reinforce the participation of youth in dialogue between the two cultures.

The film also highlighted a special session that was held at the National Dialogue Center that encouraged frank discussions and further debate. The young delegates had the opportunity to discuss matters of mutual concern and controversial issues including the concept of *jihad*, Islamic jurisprudence, racism, extremism, the consequences of Islamophobia and the threat of terrorism.

The meetings were very constructive, and the dialogue between the Saudi and British groups demonstrated their willingness to build trust and understanding, erase misconceptions and dispel negative attitudes.

In Riyadh, the workshops developed more detailed plans of joint projects between the participating organizations. They were both ambitious and constructive. The Mouth That Roars, Fainak and the Youth Empowerment organizations joined efforts to propose the "Our Everyday Lives Project," which celebrates Saudi and British cultures through film and photography. The European Alternatives, Effat University, The National Dialogue Center and The British Youth Council came up with "Active Students in Dialogue." The objective was to develop a multilingual guidance manual to build relationships among students at universities in the UK and Saudi Arabia.

The youth of both countries showed great potential and the project was a great success.

The Ministry of foreign Affairs continues to promote youth diplomacy and to encourage youth participation. The objective of the project is to further King Abdullah's intercultural dialogue initiative and to foster better relations between young Saudis and youth in other parts of the world.

Dr. Yousef Alsadoun, undersecretary for Economic and Cultural Affairs at the Ministry of Foreign Affairs, is the head of the Youth Diplomacy Project. He has launched an ambitious plan to lead and mentor young Saudis in official youth delegations to different countries to deliver a message of peace, friendship and mutual understanding. Initially the project included visits to six leading countries — China, Brazil, Germany, India, Korea and Russia

The objective of the diplomatic project was to provide the young participants an opportunity to explore new countries, learn from the experience of others and reach out with a message of peace and hope for a better future. At the end of each visit the young participants of both countries would jointly draft two letters, one to their leaders outlining their recommendations to serve their community and the other to the Secretary General of the United Nations to serve humanity.

Saudi Chinese Youth Forum

It all began in China with a delegation of 20 young Saudi boys and girls in 2010 both to mark 20 years of diplomatic relations between the People's Republic of China and Saudi Arabia and to promote King Abdullah's initiative of intercultural dialogue. The young Saudi delegation was hosted by the All-China Youth Federation, which organized a rich program that included visits to universities, cultural centers and tours of three major cities in China.

The group had an opportunity to explore historic sites in China, and learn about the ancient Chinese culture. They visited the Great Wall of China and Beijing's Forbidden City. They went to see the Museum of Qin dedicated to the terra cotta warriors, China's most ancient city, Xian and the Xian Opera House where they watched the Tang dynasty music and dance troupe perform. The youngsters also visited the ancient Mosque in Xian that was constructed by Arab merchants in 742 during the Tang dynasty. The trip was a great lesson in history and a very rich cultural experience.

The program included visits to universities where the young Saudi delegates had round table discussions and shared their views and experiences with Chinese students to promote friendship and mutual understanding. The dialogue, which talked about their aspirations and common concerns,was very enriching for both sides.

The trip ended in the city of Shanghai where participants met with Chinese colleagues at Fudan University and delivered two letters, one addressed to the Custodian of the Two Holy Mosques, King Abdullah; and Chinese President, Ho Jin Tao; and the other to UN Secretary General Ban Ki Moon. Both letters expressed hope for a global future of peace, understanding and prosperity.

The participants in their joint address to the two leaders of China and Saudi Arabia outlined their desire to build economic cooperation by initiating a Saudi-Chinese sustainable business development center that would promote small and medium-size enterprises from both countries to expand more diverse partnerships, thereby giving young people the opportunity to create their own jobs and reduce the unemployment problem prevalent in both countries.

Saudi Brazilian Youth Program

A Saudi youth delegation visited Brazil in 2011. The participants had an opportunity to visit Rio de Janeiro and explored the Amazon rain forest. They had a rich experience and a fruitful dialogue with young Braziliansduring which they discussed their respective challenges and exchanged views on youth related issues.

In the letter addressed to the two leaders of their countries the Saudi and Brazilian participants called on their leaders to create a joint center of excellence, which focused on research and development of better slum management, in order to improve the socio- economic level of their communities.

The young participants highlighted three main aspects to boost bilateral relations and cooperation between the two countries: education that could be developed through student and academic exchange programs and projects. They were:joint research in technology; youth cooperation in cultural, political and business relations; and finally providing job internships and volunteer work at major events.

They also urged their leaders to support the establishment of global Youth forums that would complement the UN's annual youth meetings and encourage stronger dialogue between countries for a better future.

Saudi Youth Outline Their Experience in Germany

The young group that visited Germany focused its discussions on renewable energy and climate change. They returned with a sense of appreciation for knowledge and a better understanding of the world.

The 10-day forum split between Hamburg and Berlin in November 2011 under the theme of "Climate Policy and Renewable Energy" was a good opportunity for the young Saudi delegation to gain experience and inspired them to be part of the global community and work hard to preserve the Earth. They realized how, as citizens of the earth, they all face the same challenges namely, climate change and pollution.

The two teams came up with ambitious proposals to the leaders of the two countries, to collaborate in the area of renewable energy. Germany would transfer knowledge on renewable energy to Saudi Arabia, and in return the Kingdom would extend solar energy across the MENA region and Europe. They also proposed the creation ofunited youth institutions to promote sustainable development and shape the new world order.

Saudi Indian youth forum

The Saudi Indian Youth forum was number four in the series of youth initiatives to promote world peace and dialogue among followers of different religions and cultures.

After five days of meetings, discussions and field trips to advanced scientific and technological centers, the young Saudi and Indian delegates proposed joint solutions in the medical, scientific and technological fields to offer services to remote regions with the help of advanced technology and e-health services.

In a message to the UN Secretary General Ban Ki Moon they outlined impressive proposals that showed intelligence and in-depth thinking. The joint message included a proposal to build an online portal, which aims to provide volunteers with programs according to their level of education to facilitate their proper service and give everyone a chance to make a change. They alsoproposed theestablishment of an E-commerce platformon the Internet(Kawthar.org)to provide the needy with basics such as food, medication and clothing. The proposal also recommended:

- e-learning centers to spread education toremote and under-privileged areas and helpconnect people with various academic institutions thus enabling them to further their education at a distance and offer them a life of dignity and enlightenment
- Tele-med programs offering affordable quality healthcare services through tele-medicine and video conferencing
- A telemedicine channel to serve remote communities around the world by sending health advice messages and getting immediate access to reliable health care services that would provide better diagnoses and treatment for patients wherever they maybe.

The participants concluded their letter with a call to the youth of all countries to come together as peace advocates and make this world a better place free of nuclear weapons and free of nuclear waste.

Dr. Yusuf Alsadun,undersecretary at the Saudi Foreign Ministry for Economic and Cultural Affairs and head of the Saudi Youth Delegation to India, said that the visit was both an educational and a diplomatic mission. The young Saudi delegation was introduced to India's diverse and ancient culture. The trip focused on building friendships and boosting cooperation in the fields of communications,IT and learning from the global experience of the Indian experts. The trip also provided an opportunity for both countries to exchange views on youth-related issues.

Modern Society and the Traditional Family

Saudi researchers continue to warn against the rise in juvenile crime among Saudis. This prompted the Makkah Governorate to take part in a major awareness campaign across the 12 regions of the province in order to curb the increase in crime. Director of Public Rights in the governorate Abdullah Al-Qarrash for example has said that the awareness campaign is aimed at addressing a deep-rooted social culture that considers the possession of arms a source of pride. He said this culture has led to the spread of knives, swords and daggers in schools and that some students have used these weapons against each other, which has led to injury and even death.

The Makkah Governorate is leading a partnership project involving government departments, nongovernmental organizations and citizens aimed at curbing what it described as "negative phenomena" that have led to a rise in crime rates.

An in-depth analysis by the governorate revealed that, about 95 percent of these cases were direct results of the negative phenomena that have spread in a number of regions including drug abuse and trafficking, acquiring knives, swords and daggers, parental disobedience, occupation of government land, family disputes including divorce, custody of children, inheritance and failing to acknowledge other people's legal rights.

The results of the analysis and the security diagnosis confirmed the need for a partnership between the government, private organizations and citizens to undertake a massive awareness campaign across the province to prevent the spread of the phenomena.

Public misconduct and rude behavior of some youngsters is evident. Our attempts to advise or reprimand them often makes trying after receiving an aggressive and insulting reply. However, verbal reactions do not pose a danger and have been tolerated for quite some time. When reactions come in the form of an assault with a weapon, however, a more dangerous trend is afoot.

Social scientists urge parents to be proper guardians and to look after their children. Unfortunately, many families do not understand the true meaning of parenting. The loss or erosion of family values of caring, nurturing and sacrificing for one's family is very disappointing. Our children should be given priority over social frivolities, and parents must understand the consequences of their neglect and uncaring attitude.

I used to feel so disturbed watching mothers who have become so neg-ligent and were busy socializing, attending religious gatherings or other functions, completely oblivious to what was happening to their children. The younger children were left in the care of nannies, while the older ones were left to do as they please without supervision or concern. Newspaper reports about domestic helpers or nannies who have abused and tortured children under their care did not make a difference. However, the latest murder case against a nanny who decapitated the four-year-old child under her care has shocked the whole country. It has raised alarm throughout so-ciety, and families are now beginning to show more concern over the safety of their children and providing quality time and attention as opposed to relying completely on domestic helpers and nannies to raise their children.

Social scientists also address the negative trend among fathers who do not display their love or are rarely available when needed, as they are too engrossed at work or else too preoccupied with socializing and attending conferences. It was not long ago that fathers took their sons to the mosque or to visit family and friends. During lunch or dinner he would be at the head of the table, listening to his children's stories about a fight at school or a problem with the teacher, and he would offer wise guidance. Parents need to be reminded to give quality time and attention and should not be distracted from their more important role, which is loving and raising their children.

The Human Rights Society has launched a campaign to educate fathers who subject their offspring to physical abuse and raise awareness among mothers who remain silent. Officials in the Ministry of Social Affairs claim that some children have died as a result of family violence, and they urge parents not to resort to violence in order to maintain discipline.

Neglect or cruelty has made young children more violent and ill-be-haved. Parents should learn how to discipline their children with love and attention and not through abuse that causes only physical and mental harm to the helpless souls. Parents have to provide their children with a sense of comfort and security at an early age in order to curb the rising rage and violence among children.

The Makkah Governorate in partnership with governmental depart-ments, NGOs and concerned citizens has conducted in-depth research into the causes of the rise of crime among young Saudis. Imams, preachers, trib-al chiefs and educational institutions have been urged to play a bigger role to curb this menacing syndrome. Many of these crimes were the result of drug abuse, possession of arms, disobedience, family feuds and refusal to pay debts.

It is sad to see the role of the imam and the preacher diminishing. The boring sermons and the screaming voices of imams screeching into microphones do not attract the younger generation. Imams should be trained to be effective communicators and trained to impart wisdom on social and current issues that concern and affect young people's lives. Only then can the role of the mosque and the preacher be revived in the eyes of the young.

The diminishing role of the school as an institution for learning and building character is another great disappointment to our society today. Teachers are underpaid and do not command respect; their teaching skills are limited, and their worries are about their survival and not about their young charges. The absence of discipline and stricter rules in many schools leave children more vulnerable to drug addiction and criminal behavior. There is an urgency to provide better, happier teachers, healthier environments and improved facilities in our schools in order to enhance the quality of life for our children today. Schools should create a healthy environment that can influence good behavior and discipline among our precious teens.

Saudi family campaigns toward educating parents about their parental role and upgrading the level of our educators and preachers are allencouraging, and they need better recognition and more social support.

Saudi society will only prosper if our children grow up to be contributing and caring citizens. The country will only progress if the youth of all the regions equally participates in the development of our nation. The nationwide campaigns are also vital to ensure family safety and national social stability.

Fighting Depression among Saudi Youth

A new study has found that the Middle East, including Saudi Arabia, has a very large number of people who suffer from depression compared with the rest of the world.

Social workers in Saudi Arabia believe that depression among Saudi youth is mainly due to the lack of recreational activities that add color and joy to life. Many young Saudis admit to being bored, depressed and frustrated. However, lately the government has attempted to address this problem and has allowed entertainment activities to be held across the country. Al-Janadriyah and Souk Okaz are among the most celebrated festivals sponsored by the government.

Several institutions have been authorized to organize cultural and entertainment activities for the nation's youth. The Organization of Art and Theater Festivals and the Saudi Arabian Society of Culture and Arts(SASCA), continue to support and sponsor entertainment events. However, they remain chartered associations under government restrictions and control. So far SASCA has sponsored several youth initiatives to create activities and entertainment facilities around the country, particularly in Jeddah.

Among the most interesting and enterprising youth companies involved in entertainment activities is Yiji, which was launched in October 2012 at the Jeddah Youth Business Committee Exhibition. The founders,AnmarFathaldin and Bader Redwan, are keen to provide Red Sea cruises with fishing, diving and snorkelling, desert getaways, cultural nights and tours in Jeddah's Al-Balad district and other historical areas. Some of their future projects include treasure hunt competitions and beach football tournaments. Let us hope that they will continue their activities without restrictions or forced closures.

Online entertainment is also becoming increasingly popular with young people. Abdullah Mando, AnmarFathaldin and Omar Murad founded a company that produced "UTURN Entertainment" in July 2010.

Fathaldin is the co-founder of UTURN Entertainment and Redwan is a partner of "nsideOut," another popular youth event management company.

Today, UTURN's 25-member team has become well known throughout the region, including Omar Hussein, the host of "Ala Al-Tayer" and Bader Saleh, host of "EyshElly." Ala Al-Tayer shows include satirical criticism of bad decisions taken by authorities and poke fun at social ills to raise awareness among the youth about the latest developments taking place in the country. According to statistics these programs have "more than 130 million views, hundreds of thousands of subscribers and 16 ongoing shows under various categories. Last year, UTURN averaged 20-30 million viewers per month in MENA alone, while competitors like Yahoo's video services in the MENA region averaged only 13 million views a month."

Ahmed Al-Maid, a graduate of McGill University with a degree in engineering and management, is the co-founder of the upcoming mobile app KareSpot, a mobile network that aims to connect volunteers with volunteering opportunities in MENA.

YaserBakr, who hosts a sports show on YouTube, has come up with the idea of a Jeddah Comedy Club that gives a chance to aspiring comedians to practice standup comedy and new comedy routines.

In Saudi Arabia young people make up 70 percent of the population. Young Saudis today speak the language of the Internet and communicate through Facebook and YouTube. Decision makers need to understand the way youth express themselves and their way of communication in order to encourage their innovative and creative contributions toward the development of our nation.

Thousands of scholarship graduates will be returning home with degrees from universities overseas. They will be coming back after having lived and gained experience in the more-advanced countries of the world. We cannot insult their intelligence and ignore their viewpoints and aspirations. RabahHabis and Sara Almaeena, both scholarship students studying in the United States, have created an online social network (wainak.com) to connect Saudi students abroad. The network provides a platform for students to connect, collaborate, and share their experiences. It keeps them well informed about the latest youth-related issues and helps them share their ideas and opinions about matters that concern their life abroad and their future careers at home. Such talented students must not come back to a life of idleness and lost opportunities. It is time to move beyond the cosmetic changes that are taking place in Saudi Arabia today.

More needs to be done to encourage youth participation. Large investments are needed to utilize the capabilities and talents of our young people. New policies and innovative strategies are required to serve their interests and address their needs. An immediate change in our many of our regulations is necessary.

Rigid laws and regulations that restrict the creativity and innovative ideas of our youth are the reasons behind their frustration. There is a dire need for a more open society and a more responsive government that can better serve the Kingdom's youth today.

Chapter 6

WOMEN'S OUTREACH

- Global Muslim women
- Muslim Women's Parliament
- Saudi women in Atlanta Forum
- German Arab women network
- Australian Arab Women Dialogue
- Mentoring the modern Muslim woman

Global Muslim Women

The misinterpretation of Islamic teachings is among the main obstacles that deter the progress of the modern Muslim society. The debate among scholars and the lack of Muslim consensus on Islamic teachings continue to slow the progress of women and delay the pace of reforms in many Muslim countries today.

Musawah, a Malaysian-based Muslim research project, has gathered enough evidence to prove that discrimination against women in Islamic countries does not accurately reflect the teachings of the Qur'an. The project calls on Muslim governments to integrate the perspectives of traditional Islam with those of contemporary human rights. It strives to integrate Islamic teachings, universal human rights and national constitutional guarantees of equality with the realities of men and women.

In Saudi Arabia, the social debate between religious scholars and reformers continues to address the current political and civil laws applied to govern the lives and roles of women in society. There are still many laws and regulations that discriminate against women based on the assumption that women are inferior; therefore, they should never be allowed to lead or hold public office — or even have a say in decisions that affect their lives. These opinions are communicated and accepted nationwide through Friday sermons, religious teachings and schoolbooks. The new image of a more modern Saudi woman — capable, educated and a contributing member to her family and society at large — should be encouraged and promoted in our textbooks and religious sermons.

Ideas and opinions about the role of women are expressed by daily columnists, writers of literature and frequently debated on talk shows. There are those who adhere to a rigid interpretation of Islam, and there are those progressive thinkers who dispute the discriminatory rulings against women in the name of Islam. Decision makers need to address the ambiguities in the teachings of the *Ulema*, and more efforts need to be made to influence religious change to empower women and recognize their rights.

The divergent opinions among modern scholars do not help, either. Many still cling to the inherited traditional belief that women should be confined to bearing children, cooking, washing and being totally obedient and subservient to the will of the husband. There are hard-liners who still regard women as intellectually, physically and morally inferior. The society remains male-dominated; men are given absolute power, and male intellectual structures form the basic framework for thought and action.

We live in the 21st century, and the technological and industrial advancements have revolutionized our way of living. The world is changing very rapidly both economically and socially, and there are many challenges facing the average Saudi family; most obvious of all is the high cost of living. Economic necessities and social responsibilities toward our children dictate that the majority of mothers earn a living in order to provide for their families and share in the expenses to afford a life of dignity and comfort.

Women need more job opportunities and better wages to survive and support themselves and their families. When women suffer, whole families suffer. We need to bring harmony and justice to the Saudi family in order to build a progressive, healthy society. We need to bring stability to Saudi families and create a happy and less stressful environment in all Saudi homes

Social injustice against women requires appropriate and effective, codified Shariah law so that all are aware of women's legal rights and so violators can be held accountable for misdeeds.

The way to reform begins with the will to amend laws, apply a new national gender policy, and establish institutions to implement them. There must be greater representation of women at all levels of government to address women's affairs and concerns.

Social activists and reformers should seek advice from global Muslim organizations, such as Musawah and learn from their experience to implement the true teachings of Islam and influence change within Saudi society. At the same time, religious scholars need to discuss these concerns with reformers and find common ground to move this country forward. Anyone who thinks these problems can be ignored without severe economic consequences to the nation is living in a fool's paradise and forcing the rest of us to share the accommodation.

It is truly regrettable that our own men, who should be wise in such matters of justice, need to be reminded it is time to end what could be described as misinterpreting the teachings of the Prophet Muhammad (peace be upon Him) and the denial of the rights of their own mothers, wives, sisters and daughters. They need to be reminded of what the Prophet said: "The best of you are those that are best to their women-folk, and I am the best amongst you to my family."

It is time for Saudi women to join hands with their sisters in Islam who seek to end discrimination against women and publicly reclaim Islam's spirit of justice for all.

Muslim Women's Parliament

An international group of 200 women who attended the 2009 Women's Islamic Initiative in Spirituality and Equality (WISE) conference in the Malaysian capital of Kuala Lumpur truly inspired a movement for global justice. During the four days of fruitful sessions, the WISE women debated and discussed global issues of concern to Muslim women today.

Many scholars presented research papers and case studies that portrayed the sorry situation of Muslim women discriminated against in the name of Islam. One of the interesting sessions was an open forum called "Chair Chai Chats" in which participants discussed topics of interest to Muslim women. I was asked to lead one of these forums and share my experiences as a woman journalist in Saudi Arabia dedicated to addressing gender issues, creating awareness about the legal rights of women in Islam and exposing discrimination against women in a male-dominated society.

After an hour-and-a-half of discussions and heated debate, which centered around Saudi culture and lifestyle, the diverse group of Muslim women leaders from Malaysia, Germany, Canada, Pakistan, Morocco, Jordan and the United States remained unconvinced that there is a genuine reform movement in Saudi Arabia and that many Saudis are indeed moderate and tolerant in nature.

One of the participants in a very apologetic tone told me that I was trying to portray a rosy picture of Saudi society and a more humane picture of the Saudi people, whereas many who have come for Haj and Umrah had experienced the exact opposite. Some women have been insulted in the Grand Mosque in Makkah; some Saudi men did not treat them with respect.

Another participant was critical of "the adherence to a rigid interpretation of Islam that has harmed the image of Muslims all over the world." At the end of the session, I felt frustrated because I was unable to defend the intolerant behavior of some in my country, and I could not deny the distorted ideology that many still adhere to in our part of the world.

There was a time when Muslims all over the world felt privileged to make friends or even meet people from Makkah and Medina. It is unfortunate that we are not living up to the expectations of the global Muslim community.

Another interesting session in the conference highlighted case studies from different Muslim communities in which women activists have influenced change and addressed social injustice.

One particular case study of the Muslim women in Mindanao could very well apply to the situation of women in Saudi Arabia — especially in the areas of marriage and family, economic rights, political participation and decision-making. The project was initiated based on an alliance between Muslim women advocates and Muslim religious leaders to clarify the roles of men and women in accordance with the basic teachings of the Holy Qur'an and the Sunnah. It aimed to influence Muslim religious leaders who insisted on retaining traditional, discriminatory and repressive beliefs on women.

Muslim religious leaders and social scientists conducted consultations and workshops to guarantee respect for the basic teachings of the Qur'an and Sunnah as well as human-rights principles.

The project proved to be very effective with 15 drafted *khutbas*(the primary formal occasion for public preaching, particularly at noon Prayers on Fridays)that were more progressive interpretations of the Qur'an and the Sunnah. Ultimately, a handbook was produced for imams to use during Friday sermons and marriage counselling.

For example, the sermons on early marriages declared that Islam clarifies important requirements before marriage can take place, which include the age of maturity or capacity to distinguish right from wrong, mental capability, emotional preparation, physical grounding, financial capability and, most importantly, the consent of the concerned parties.

The sermons on violence against women affirmed that all forms of violence against women must be eradicated, for so long as women suffer abuses, women cannot achieve their full potential as free and equal members of society.

The project also included training program for women religious leaders, giving them initial training on delivery of advice based on the core messages of 15 prepared sermons on gender-inequality issues. Saudi religious scholars should consider adopting this strategy to create a more tolerant environment for women in this country

The session on empowering women as peace advocates was the most moving and the most powerful event of the conference. A documentary about the struggle of women in Liberia was heartbreaking but at the same time most inspiring. It delivered a very powerful message of peace and recognized the vital role of women in peacemaking and conflict resolution.

The conference hosted many women from war zones such as Palestine, Afghanistan, Iraq, Pakistan and Kenya who shared the stories of their struggles. Many of them definitely took home an experience that could empower them to act as peacemakers, although the peace they seek may be more difficult to attain.

During the closing session participants pledged to support a movement of *Jihad* Against Violence as part of the Muslim women's struggle for peace, and a group of women scholars and activists formed a global Muslim women's Shoura Council to promote women's rights within an Islamic framework through education and advocacy.

There are many lessons to be learned from such conferences. Saudi Arabia should encourage and host such a conference in order to support Muslim women's initiatives for peace and social justice. Saudi women could also use the support of their sisters in Islam; they can no longer afford to live in isolation from the rest of the global Muslim community.

Moreover, the Kingdom is now challenged more than ever before to take a more affirmative role and act as the true leader of the Muslim world.

Business Opportunities Forum in Atlanta

Not many people outside our borders are aware of the existence of exceptional women in Saudi Arabia, so the presence of highly qualified women was a great surprise to a lot of participants at the US Saudi Business Opportunities Forum held in Atlanta from Dec. 5-7, 2011.

The participation of highly competent and professional Saudi women certainly contributed to the success of the event. The Saudi Committee for International Trade (CIT) organizedthe forum together with US-Saudi Arabian Business Council and Saudi-US Trade Group in collaboration with the Saudi Ministry of Commerce and Industry and the US Commercial Service.

The Saudi women who took part in the forum were certainly an impressive demonstration of commercial and intellectual ability and were:

- Lubna Al-Olayan delivered the keynote speech with great eloquence. In her opening remarks, she brilliantly summarized the geopolitical challenges that the US and Saudi Arabia face today and gave an optimistic view of the future cooperation between the two countries. Lubna Olayan is a highly experienced financial leader and globally known. She is the CEO of Olayan Co., a private multinational enterprise. She was named by Time magazine as one of the 100 most influential people in the world, and she sits on many boards and councils because of her extensive experience and expertise in corporate finance, international banking, distribution and manufacturing.

- Her sister,Hutham Olayan, moderated the session on opportunities for finance and investment with equal professionalism. She leads the Olayan Group's activities in the Americas and has been elected to the board of directors of Morgan Stanley. She leads an organization that manages a diversified portfolio of US public and private equities and real estate based in New York. She is a founding member of the Arab Bankers Association of North America, a trustee of the conference board and a board member of the Institute for International Economics.

- Dr. Hanan Balkhy, executive director for infection control at the National Guard Hospital, moderated the panel of health and medical services. She represented the Saudi doctors well known in the field of medical research and health care.

- Dr. SalwaAlhazaa, professor of ophthalmology at Alfaisal University and head and consultant of ophthalmology, senior clinical scientist and consultant in genetics at King Faisal Specialist Hospital and Research Center, gave an informative presentation in the panel discussing building the health-care sector through innovation and technology. Her logic and research findings impressed the audience.

- Dr. Alhazaa also participated in the outreach program to foster better relations with American women in business. The participants included outstanding Saudi women in the field of architecture, finance, information technology and entrepreneurship.

- SamraAlkuwaiz, a financial expert and lecturer at King Saud University is a board member and partner of Osool Capital in Riyadh. She has often been named among the most influential women in the region's financial industry. Alkuwaiz has encouraged many Saudi women to participate in finance, invest in the stock market and build portfolios.

- NadyaBakhurji founded her own architectural consultancy company, Riwaq. This was the first company to be owned by a woman. It is registered under the Saudi Council of Engineers. She is also the first Saudi woman to become a board member of the Saudi Council of Engineers and has campaigned for the recognition of Saudi female architects and engineers in the Kingdom.
- Nouf Alrakan is CEO of Alimtiaz Alamthal Trading Co. specializing in IT solutions, clothing and food products. She has also established a new company representing the oil and gas industry in the Kingdom and embarked on setting up a manufacturing facility.
- Khadija Koshak leads a successful fashion-design business. She joined the program with her aspiring daughter who is currently studying communications in the US. Together they presented a bright picture of two generations of educated and greatly accomplished Saudi women.

The outreach initiative was one of the highlights of the Atlanta Forum where some of the most dynamic American female executives and entrepreneurs met with the delegation of professional Saudi women in a round table discussion aimed at promoting women in global business. In an open and frank dialogue, the Saudi women discussed issues concerning their negative image in the international community and projected an accurate picture of Saudi women. Saudi women, they said, have their own hopes and aspire to contribute to the progress and development of their society.

The forum concluded with a commitment to recognize the great potential of Saudi career women and to explore new business opportunities between the two countries.

At the end of the session, the hosts offered the Saudi delegation membership in the International Women's Forum, (IWF), a global organization where leading women of the world are united in a network to promote better world leadership with new ideas and perspectives to make our world a better place. With great enthusiasm the Saudi women welcomed the opportunity to gain experience from the IWF to better serve their governments, corporations and academic institutions.

The Saudi women maintained it was time they came out of their isolation and become global partners contributing to intercultural understanding, peace and global prosperity. They hoped that this dialogue would be the beginning of a long-term relationship between the American and Saudi women business communities.

The international community can facilitate Saudi women's participation and allow their contribution in joint projects between faith-based networks or humanitarian organizations. Their participation in initiatives that address global concerns would create a greater impact in fostering international understanding of the Muslim way of life. When given the chance women could play a more effective role by building trust and eliminating the elements of fear and suspicion that divide our world

The CIT should be commended for their brave initiative to include a delegation of accomplished Saudi women in the forum. No doubt, the presence of highly qualified women had a strong impact and contributed to the success of the forum.

Muslim organizations should sponsor more of these events to erase the Western misconceptions of Saudi women and encourage our capable women to excel and participate in global events to showcase their capabilities and willingness to contribute and develop the planet around them.

German- Arab Women Network

The EU is stepping up pressure on companies and governments in Europe, threatening a legally binding quota if companies fail to increase the number of women in top positions.

Gender discrimination in the workplace is still a subject of debate in the more advanced countries of the world, in spite of global and national laws and regulations that prohibit the discrimination against women in business and the workforce. Even in Germany,where the German Chancellor is a woman, prominent businesswomen still suffer from discrimination more than in any other European country.

The situation of women in business and in the workplace was the focus of discussions during the First German-Arab Women's Network Forum, "Leading Women for Sustainable Economic Growth," held under the patronage of HRH Princess Umayyad BintAl Hassan on April 12, 2012, in Hamburg. Arab and German women shared their experiences and exchanged views regarding the position of women in business and in public life.

The eloquent opening statements of German officials were strong messages indicating that these women mean business ,and that they will not put up with any morediscrimination.

The Second Mayor of Hamburg Dr. Dorothee Stapelfeldt in her opening comments stressed the need to promote the role of women in order to serve the economy, the family and society at large. She said that gender discrimination was a recognized global problem in the workforce. However all countries were obligated by international law to reduce it. To do so, she said, we needed to educate people about the negative impact of discrimination. Diversity in styles and approaches could add more value and increase productivity. Companies must recognize the capabilities of the qualified and professional women and their vital role to lead society towards a better future.

Eva-Maria Welskop-Deffaa, chair of the department for equality at the German Ministry for Women, spoke on the need to provide women with equal wages and equal opportunities in both governmental and nongovernmental sectors. She said the German women were qualified and had a sense of responsibility. However, they were still limited in their contributions because of the prevailing discriminatory trend in leading German companies. As a result there is growing demand for the implementation of a quota system that would guarantee top positions for women in leading German companies and government positions.

Arab women representatives from Jordon, Egypt, Morocco and Saudi Arabia all agreed that women in Arab countries shared the same fate if not worse. They were marginalized and struggling to implement laws and regulations to end discrimination against them socially and economically.

Reem Barghouty Damen, chairwoman of the Jordan Forum for business and professional women who presented the greeting statements on behalf of the Jordanian Princess, shared the role of her organization to advance the interest of women through strategic partnerships with NGOs and international organizations in order to create a proactive societal role for Jordanian women. She said the Jordanian Forum has been very active in addressing discriminatory issues that hinder the participation of women in business and the work place; however much more needed to be done to achievethe desired goals.

Haifa Al Kaylani, founder and chairwoman of the International Women's Forum, (AIWF) described the initiatives of her organization to champion the advancement of gender equality and sustainable development in the Arab world with partners committed to meet the challenges of the future.

She highlighted AIWF's wider reach of advocacy work with an objective to create public awareness of women's potentials and achievements and linking Arab women in 22 countries with each other and with their counterparts in the international communityto promote the role of women in the Arab World.

Prof.Dr. Dina Shokry, from the Mediterranean Academy of Forensic Sciences in Egypt spoke about the Arab spring and the active role of women in the workforce and in Government. They had assumed leadership roles in all fields and many had worked hard to serve their community. As a doctor, she has been very active in addressing domestic violence and social discrimination. She spoke about effective awareness campaigns that support women who were victims of domestic violence and afraid to report spousal abuse.

The Forum also listened to the unique experiences of Saudiwomen who had shown great determination to gain higher qualifications and succeed in many sectors of society. They continue to work hard to break the glass ceiling that has prevented them from achieving higher-level positions in Government and in the workplace.

The Arab and German women discussed the quota system and new laws and regulationsto elevate more women to higher positions in government and in business. Some Arab countries have successfully introduced quotas, like Morocco and Jordan.Perhaps Arab women also need to join German women'scalls for quotas to guarantee executive and higher positions.Saudi women could certainly benefit by gaining more seats in the municipal and consultative councils.

The network Forum provided an excellent opportunity for German and Arab women to exchange common goals and best practices for a better society.It attracted a large number of leading businesswomen in Hamburg who were eager to learn about Arab women culture and way of life.

The Euro-Mediterranean Association organized the event for Cooperation and Development (EMA). This is an organization, headquartered in Hamburg, which advocates the interdisciplinary deepening of economic cooperation and the enhancement of intercultural understanding between Germany, North Africa, the Middle East and the GCC countries (EMA-region). With a young and very dynamic team as well as high-ranking board members — such as HRH Prince Hassan bin Talal as EMA's President of Honor, EMA plays a special role in Germany for the promotion of the German-Arab dialogue.

The participation of professional Arab women in such events can contribute towards erasing the negative stereotypes of Middle Eastern women and enhance economic cooperation and intercultural understanding between European countries and the Arab world.

The Australian Arab women Dialogue

The Australian Arab women Dialogue was an opportunity for the participants to find common grounds and discuss solutions to some of the mutual problems and concerns that Australian and Arab women face today. Discrimination and Violence against women and their children was a topic of mutual concern. It dominated many of the round table discussions during which the Arab women were able to learn about the Australian National Plan to stop discrimination and violence against women and their children. The Arab women were inspired by the Australian Women in leadership positions who have supported the National Plan to address the problem. It includes all government departments working in unity to put an end to the violence and to guarantee a safe community for women and their children. It focuses on prevention and holding perpetrators accountable. The Australian National plan succeeded in changing attitudes and behaviors that tolerate violence against women and reducing economic, social and political inequalities between men and women. It has played a great role in reducing violence against women in Australia. It has also helped in creating more positive inclusive and safe communities and equal and respectful relationships.

The Australian National Plan to stop discrimination and violence against women and their children targeted schools, communities, sporting groups and the media. It addressed the negative social norms as well as aggressive individual attitudes. One of the most interesting initiatives that was of great interest to the Arab participants was the White Ribbon campaign which was introduced to raise awareness among men and boys and educate them about the roles they can play to prevent discrimination and violence against women.

The majority of men are non violent, but they need to be supported to speak out against the violence against women. Organizations such as the white Ribbon Foundation of Australia have made progress in this area, however Australian women like many women in the Arab countries feel more can be done to put an end to the phenomena that is still prevalent.

Changing and shaping attitudes and behaviors of young people is critical to preventing violence against women in the future. More should be done to encourage more men to speak out against violence and promote non-violence. It is important to expand men's knowledge and skills in sustaining respectful relationships.

The women all agreed that boys should be educated at an young age to respect women . Education is an important means that can help people develop and maintain non violent and respectful relationships. School and community cultures need to support and foster structural and individual change. School based approaches that help young people identify in appropriate sexual or violent behavior , and shape their expectations and capacity to build and sustain respectful relationships, are promising examples of primary prevention that appear to be working internationally. Children learn their attitudes and behavior from those around them. Moreover it has been proven that positive adult roles could encourage young people to develop positive respectful relationships.

The representatives of the eight Arab countries were all eager to adopt the White Ribbon campaign and implement it in their countries. They all agreed that the international campaign should gain more prominence in Arab countries to change the negative attitudes towards women. More Arab men should be involved in addressing the discrimination and violence against women in the Arab world.

In Saudi Arabia King Abdullah has played a leading role in supporting women and has defied extremists who discriminate against women and are insensitive to the violence committed against them. Prince Alwaleed Bin Talal has championed the role of women and supported many programs to protect women's rights and status in society. Prominent lawyers and Shoura council members are beginning to speak out against the negative attitudes against women that encourages the violence against them. Men in Media such as Khaled Almaeena the Editor in Chief of the Saudi Gazette and prominent writer Abdullah Al-Alami continue to speak out against discrimination against women and are always exposing the perpetrators who get away with minimum or no punishments for their violent behavior. However we need more of these examples to reduce the violence against women in our society.

It is time we adopt the international White Ribbon campaign and the Australian National Plan to reduce Violence against Women which also includes innovative social marketing campaigns to change attitudes and behaviors that contribute to violence against women and a national Sexual Assault, Domestic and family violence Counseling Service, an Office for Women to increase women's economic security and ensuring women's equal place in society and a center for the study of sexual Assault and an institute of family studies.

The exchange of ideas, initiatives and strategies between Arab women and the experts among Australian women could create positive outcomes and support the endeavors of Arab women to build a safer environment and a better future for their loved ones.

Mentoring the Modern Muslim woman

Saudi Women in International Organizations was the theme of a meeting that gathered together more than 150 professional women in Jeddah to celebrate the launch of CellA+, a nonprofit organization of Saudi professional women under the umbrella of Al-Nahda Women's Philanthropic Society.

Al-Nahda is celebrating 50 years of service toward the empowerment of Saudi women through financial and social support. The society has provided training and employment for women to help them become active partners in the development of their society.

CellA+ serves as a link for idea sharing and networking for business and professional women across the country. The team of professional women has come together to provide support for other professionals who wish to develop skills in their fields of work and to provide opportunities and share resources in order to empower CellA+ members.

Dr. ThorayaObaid, the executive director of the United Nations Population Fund and former undersecretary general of the United Nations, gave an inspiring presentation in which she shared her long and rich experience at the UN. She stressed the importance of education and mentoring programs that can have a strong impact on communities. She said she has always believed it to be her responsibility to mentor future leaders and said that women in particular have a more important role to play in helping other women, emphasizing the need for increased empowerment of women across the country.

Dr. Obaid became the first Saudi woman to receive a government scholarship to study at a university in the United States; she is also the first

Saudi woman to head a United Nations agency. She was rated among the 50 most powerful Arab women by Forbes magazine in 2004 and profiled as one of the 100 Muslim Builders of World Civilization and Culture in Notable Muslims, by the deputy editor for The Encyclopedia of the Islamic World and editor for The Oxford Dictionary of Islam in 2006. She has won many international awards and has been honored by many academic and global organizations.

Dr. Obaid is a great example of a role model who commands respect and promotes the image of the contemporary Saudi woman who can contribute toward the development of her country. She shared her experience in managing a large organization with many employees and explained how an atmosphere of friendship and collaboration can increase productivity and make a difference in any organization. She has set high standards for success and highlighted the need for professionalism to produce better leaders for the community.

King Abdullah's reform movement has raised the status of women locally and internationally. Islam has granted women rights that need to be instilled within our society. A more-balanced partnership between men and women in accordance with the true Shariah law can strengthen the position of the contemporary woman in Saudi society and allow her to turn her challenges into achievements.

Progressive and qualified women are more eager to become official members of the Shoura Council and to participate in municipal councils They will finally have a voice in the decision making process. The contemporary professional woman can no longer be isolated. Today she is included in official state delegations, attends international conferences and contributes toward national and global scientific research to serve humanity. However, there are still many challenges, and the contemporary woman is still struggling with local attempts to marginalize her role.

Rigid customs and traditions and incorrect interpretations of Islamic law continue to curb her freedom to contribute and excel.

The role of organizations like CellA+ and Al-Nahda society is crucial. They can be instrumental in empowering women through their networking support and professional advice and awareness campaigns.

Mentoring programs can help us produce role models who can project the image of the contemporary Muslim woman who commands respect and qualifies for leadership positions and roles in international organizations.

Our society has a lack of positive role models, and there is a dire need for effective initiatives to provide proper mentoring to guide our young professionals in their careers and ensure a more prosperous future for our nation. There should be a nationwide Role Model Program that can provide positive examples for our youth who are in need of hope, self-confidence, inspiration and guidance to succeed. Our children need role models to look up to in order to embrace change and adopt a more modern lifestyle in which women are treated with the same respect that is offered to men.

There are many international role model programs that could be applied in our schools. Community Classroom Visit Programs produce caring adults who become role model volunteers, capable of inspiring young women and providing life skills to help them achieve academic excellence, set ambitious goals for their future, and ultimately enable them to become contributing citizens.

Every woman who is in a leadership position today has an obligation to act as a role model and be a source of strength within her community. She should support women's contributions and actively participate in public life. The contemporary professional woman today can be a powerful force for change if she is given the opportunity to be an effective partner in the development of this nation.

Chapter 7

Global Dialogue

- Obama's outreach to Muslims
- Coalition preaches mutual respect
- Dialogue of Abrahamic Faiths
- GCC, Dialogue and Islamophobia
- Interfaith dialogue promoting universal principles of tolerance
- Business investments promote cultural understanding
- Moderation and peaceful coexistence
- Lessons from the Egyptian Revolution
- Australia takes a new stand on Palestine

Obama's Outreach to Muslims

US President Barack Obama was very eloquent in his speech to the Arab and Muslim world. He addressed seven major issues that are of major concern to all Arabs and Muslims. However, the first two issues are the main sources of tension and are obstacles to peace, mainly America's policy toward Islam and its policy toward the Arab/Israeli conflict.

The American president's address indicated a new policy that would reverse the negative attitude toward Muslims. "I have come here to seek a new beginning between the United States and the Muslim world," he said, and acknowledged Muslim contributions and showed genuine good will when he stated, "America is not — and never will be — at war with Islam."

These words were well received by Muslims everywhere who wereeager to see an end to the war that was waged on Islam by George W. Bush. For eight years Bush's administration adopted a policy of applying collective guilt on all Muslims and conducted a smear campaign against Muslim ideology and way of life. This angered and alienated Muslims and caused America tolose allies in the Arab and Muslim world. Obama promised to reverse this policy and said, "I consider it part of my responsibility as president of the United States to fight against negative stereotypes of Islam wherever they appear." This statement was highly appreciated and commanded great respect and trust for the president from the majority in the Muslim world.

Obama also promised an end to the cycle of suspicion and discord that was generated by false accusations and distorted information of the Bush administration. Referring to the trauma of 9/11, he said: "The fear and anger that it provoked ... in some cases, it led us to act contrary to our ideals.

We are taking concrete actions to change course. I have unequivocally prohibited the use of torture by the US, and I have ordered the prison at Guantanamo Bay closed by early next year."

Again this was another statement that could help us erase the painful memory of the innocent who were dragged to Guantanamo from all over the world or the humiliation of the proud Iraqi people at the hands of American soldiers in Abu Ghraib.

Obama later spoke about another source of tension, "the situation between Israelis, Palestinians and the Arab world." However, this was where Obama lost the hearts and minds of many Arabs and Muslims. He was right when he said that, "No single speech can eradicate years of mistrust," but neglected to add, and years of abuse and deception.

Obama lost many of us when he chose to stress that, "the Palestinians must abandon violence," but omitted to show any condemnation of Israeli atrocities and war crimes. Instead he described Palestinians' legitimate resistance as violence, which he thinks would lead to a dead end. He said, "It is a sign of neither courage nor power to shoot rockets at sleeping children, or blow up old women on a bus." Again we were reminded of the continued American double standards and American insensitivity to the killings of women and children in Gaza and the Palestinian territory.

What about Israeli use of lethal weapons and the destruction of Palestinian homes and schools? What about Israeli use of F-16 fighter planes and Apache helicopters to slay a wheelchair-bound cripple or to deliberately target Gaza schools and bakeries?

President Obama also should realize that it is neither a sign of courage nor equitable justice to keep thousands of innocent women and children in jails for many years and deprive them of their freedom and dignity. It is inhumane and against all human rights to evict a people from their lands and destroy their homes, deprive them of food and water and leave them to die a slow death without medical help or proper sanitation.

Which situation deserves more sympathy and attention?

Clearly Obama has demonstrated once again that the American bias toward Israel will never stop and that the US can never be an honest broker in this conflict. The US president said that Hamas must put an end to violence, recognize past agreements and recognize Israel's right to exist. If he is really a man of his word and is genuinely working for a peaceful solution he also should have said Israel must likewise put an end to violence, recognize UN resolutions 242 and 338, to which the US is signatory, and abandon its expansionist plans. Israel must understand that Palestinians are there to stay, and they will not abandon their homeland. The new American administration must also recognize that the Muslim people's bond with Palestinians will continue to grow with or without US support. This bond is unbreakable and is based upon religious, cultural and historical ties and that the aspiration for a Palestinian state is rooted in a religious and historical conviction that cannot be denied.

Having said that the majority of the Arab and Muslim states will continue to pursue peace and support the Arab peace initiative, Obama reiterated that the US does not accept the legitimacy of continued Israeli settlements, and he stressed that the only way to end the Arab-Israeli conflict is through a two-state solution where Israelis and Palestinians live in peace and security.

There are still many questions that demand clear answers. Can Obama fulfill his promise to put an end to Israeli violence and expansion? Will the US continue to supply sophisticated weaponry and vetoes that support Israel? Will there be more positive American policies toward the Middle East and the Muslim world? Many Muslims are still very skeptical and have little faith in America's will to resolve the Arab-Israeli conflict. They remain wary of President Obama's ability to halt Israel's atrocities and deliver peace to the Middle East.

The majority of Muslims believe that there is a genuine desire by Obama and many noble people in the West to put an end to Islamophobia. Nevertheless there are many Muslims who still feel threatened by American extremists who continue to demonize Islam and Muslims. It is very evident that there is a greater need to foster interfaith relations and build bridges of understanding between Muslim societies and the West. Saudi Arabia is leading this campaign and promoting King Abdullah's initiative of interfaith Dialogue.

Coalition preaches mutual respect

The interfaith dialogue initiated by Custodian of the Two Holy Mosques King Abdullah to build bridges of understanding between Islam and the West has been well received by religious leaders worldwide. This was evident at the community outreach program that was organized by the Council of Saudi Chambers of Commerce and Industry's Committee of International Trade (CIT) on the sidelines of the US-Saudi Business Opportunities Forum April 28-29, 2010, in Chicago.

Five members of the delegation accompanying Commerce and Industry Minister Abdullah ZainalAlireza to the Windy City participated in the Interfaith Breakfast Dialogue, which took place at the University of Chicago's Gleacher Center. They got the opportunity to discover the efforts of religious leaders dedicated to building a peaceful coexistence between the Abrahamic faiths in the Chicago community.

In a moderated panel discussion, five religious leaders of different faiths addressed the backlash after 9/11 and stressed the need for interfaith programs to dispel misunderstanding and media misconceptions that spread hatred and false information about different faiths. The panel included an imam, a reverend, a rabbi and other religious leaders who outlined their missions toward finding common grounds and building trust and respect among all religions.

They also shared their experiences and activities involving the Chicago community in interfaith dialogue and interfaith learning. One of the most interesting institutions represented was The Chicago Coalition for Inter-Religious Learning, a group of Catholics, Jews and Muslims working together with an approach based on a spirit of respectful inquiry, neither attempting to "convert" people nor claiming that there is no difference between the three Abrahamic religions.

Indeed, this new approach of accepting and respecting the differences between Muslims, Christians and Jews could put an end to hostilities and eliminate the tension and conflict that mars relations between the Muslim world and the West. The coalition includes educators, writers and book publishers who came together after 9/11 to confront teachings of hatred, contempt and damaging stereotypes that can be found in religious school classrooms.

It is truly heartening to know that there are efforts to stop the spread of Islamophobia and discrimination against people of different faiths. The religious leaders of Chicago are engaged in organizing interactive workshops and giving presentations to religious school educators and administrators to stimulate inter-religious thinking and to create better teaching models. Moreover, they are developing a more accurate multimedia resource guide, and they are supporting student participation in trilateral dialogue activities and other interfaith learning projects.

Among their main activities is the monitoring of publications, films and other classroom resources for coalition members to review or endorse. They plan to put the bibliographical information and reviews on their website as a resource guide and a reliable database. In addition, the group emphasizes the need for sensitive, interfaith children's books and plans a series of teachers' guides for interfaith education.

Through interfaith learning, the coalition strives to enable all to understand the different religious beliefs and at the same time allow all to remain true to the core of their own religious traditions. These noble initiatives should be implemented on a global scale, and they should be publicized in order to promote friendly relations and goodwill between the United States and the Muslim world.

The Q&A session that followed the presentations of the panelists was another opportunity for the members of the Saudi delegation to share their concerns and outline King Abdullah's interfaith dialogue initiative, which is based on mutual respect and peaceful coexistence. The Saudis stressed that religious leaders should not follow the paths of their predecessors who fought many wars over religion. Today, the global community should be more concerned with eradicating poverty and disease, protecting the environment, ending wars and eliminating the injustices and human suffering that still exist in many parts of the world.

At the end of the visit, the men and women of the Saudi delegation said they appreciated the initiatives of this noble coalition and felt comfortable over the fact that there are partners in America who are now genuine in their efforts to build bridges of understanding and eager to put an end to the demonization of Islam and Muslims in the United States.

The mission of Commerce and Industry Minister Abdullah ZainalAlireza, who led a delegation of finance and petroleum ministers and 200 business leaders, academics and media personalities to build stronger relations and friendly ties with the US, certainly has been a great success. It has opened a new page in Saudi-American relations, and it has paved the way to end the misconceptions that have created the tensions between the two countries.

Saudi Arabia continues its moderate and peaceful policies, combating terrorism and fighting extremism. It is reaching out to the whole world to implement trade relations and promote global prosperity. Let us hope that peaceful partners and allies — as well as religious leaders — will continue to hold on to a spirit of goodwill and mutual respect in order to regain the peace of the world and build a better future for our younger generation.

Dialogue of Abrahamic Faiths

Muslim countries need to establish business partnerships and support joint projects between faith-based organizations in order to foster better relations between Muslim communities and the West. The interfaith dialogue initiated by King Abdullah needs to be given better attention by Saudi and international Muslim organizations. More efforts need to be exerted to reach out to faith-based organizations to address the challenges of the 21st century.

Exploring what the Abrahamic faiths have in common was the theme of an interfaith dialogue held on Dec.9. 2011,at Atlanta's All Saints Episcopal Church on the sidelines of the recent US-Saudi Business Opportunities Forum. The Saudi Committee of International Trade (CIT) and the Saudi-US Trade Group organized the event.

Nick Stuart, president of Odyssey Networks, America's largest interfaith media organization, moderated the discussion. The American panelists were prominent religious leaders in Atlanta; the southeast regional director of Anti-Defamation League, president of the Concerned Black Clergy, president of the Alliance for Christian Media, and dean of the Chapel and Religious Life at Emory University. Saudi participants included senior members of the CIT.

The dialogue focused on two major global concerns of this century, poverty and the environment. The discussion was very informative, and the participants exchanged their experiences in dealing with these two realities that are threatening our world. They debated the theological aspects of the three religions and shared the actual spiritual practices in their daily lives that reinforce the commonalities of Abrahamic beliefs.

The dialogue ended with five recommendations for future interfaith projects: The need to build trust, address issues with open transparency, acquire knowledge and understanding of the other faiths, and to come up with joint projects that could serve their communities and tackle common issues of major concern.

Meanwhile, the outreach program succeeded in connecting the Saudi business leaders with the Odyssey Media Networks, which supplies videos of interfaith news stories to CNN, Huffington Post and a number of websites run by hosts such as AOL. It has its own website and mobile app, Call on Faith (available at i-Phone and BlackBerry app stores), which carries 18 short-form video channels. One of the main contributions is providing weekly links to churches to help preachers prepare for their weekly sermons, linking faith to the weekly events that are uppermost in the lives of the faithful, such as news about the economy, the environment, poverty and how we treat each other.

One of the objectives of Odyssey Networks is to launch a similar service for Muslims in America to aid preaching and study in the mosques and linking the insights from the Qur'an and the *Hadith* to topical news stories. Muslim organizations need to reach out and connect with such sincere interfaith efforts to foster better understanding between Muslims and other faiths.

Indeed the Saudis could learn a lot from their experience and adapt some of their programs to promote the role of the mosque and make it more effective by providing realistic guidance for the faithful.

Muslim organizations certainly could learn from such experiences in order to provide proper interpretations of the Qur'an and follow the authenticated *Sunnah* that relates more to the realities of our time in order to address the challenges of the 21st century.

There are many other ways in which we can benefit from establishing links with more-experienced interfaith organizations. One of them is encouraging Muslims to reach out and interact with other faiths and engage in dialogue to correct distorted information that has harmed Muslims and has given Islam a bad name. Odyssey is trying to grow its Muslim membership, and they are interested in appointing a Muslim board member who could contribute by providing firsthand information about the true principles of Islam and give a Muslim perspective on current issues of global concern.

Other initiatives could include an internship or a sponsored Muslim video journalist who would join the production staff for a few months to interact with other professionals and learn from their experience to cover stories from the Muslim world that would provide a more accurate picture of Muslim culture and way of life.

Talented Muslims in this field could introduce Muslim insights to the production team, whether it be new media, Web expertise, graphic design or video journalists and editors.

Such initiatives need more coverage and support to build global trust and eliminate the elements of fear and suspicion that have divided the Abrahamic faiths. There is a need to establish business partnerships and support joint projects between faith-based organizations to address global challenges like poverty or the environment and other pressing issues that threaten humanity.

Muslim organizations in Saudi Arabia that support King Abdullah's initiative of interfaith dialogue need more qualified scholars and media professionals to seek interfaith initiatives emerging out of the US like the

Odyssey Networks and find ways to link up to highlight Muslim contributions that provide a positive perspective promoting peace and harmony.

The outreach program initiated by the CIT to promote an interfaith dialogue with Saudi Arabia could be the beginning of a strong partnership to foster better relations with the West and a chance to find common ground between the Abrahamic faiths. Investment in such initiatives would contribute to global peace and prosperity.

GCC, Dialogue and Islamophobia

The Ministers of the six-nation Gulf Cooperation Council (GCC) met in 2012 to promote cultural interaction and mutual understanding among themselves, while building cultural bridges to reach people of different nations, faiths and ethnicities. The meeting signifies a more positive direction towards creating a more united GCC and a determined effort to address the West's negative image of Islam and the Arab Gulf heritage.

Promoting cultural interaction and mutual understanding among the people of the Gulf can strengthen the position of the Gulf States in the region. However, social activists in the Gulf assert that the only way to achieve a stronger GCC is by activating the social debate between religious scholars and reformers to address the current political and civil laws that are applied to govern the lives of citizens and the roles of women in particular. There are still many laws based on cultural beliefs, traditions and outdated regulations that discriminate against women and are detrimental to progress, which need to be revised in order to build a stronger GCC presence in the region.

In most of the Gulf countries there are still those who adhere to a rigid interpretation of Islam, and there are those progressive thinkers who dispute the discriminatory rulings in the name of Islam. Decision makers need to address the ambiguities in the teachings of the *Ulema* and more efforts need to be made to influence a collective stand towards a moderate Islamic rule to recognize the rights of all citizens.

The way to build a more cohesive GCC begins with the will to amend laws, apply unified public policies and establish effective institutions to implement them. There must be greater representation of women at all levels of government to address women's affairs and concerns. Engaging with the young more effectively in the nation building can also help promote solidarity within the GCC.

The debate among scholars and the lack of Muslim consensus on Islamic teachings continues to undermine our image and reflect badly abroad on our culture and heritage. The GCC must play a bigger role to integrate the perspectives of traditional Islam with those of contemporary human rights. It must strive to integrate Islamic teachings, universal human rights, national constitutional guarantees of equality with the realities of men and women and provide opportunities for all citizens to better serve their governments, corporations and academic institutions. Gulf countries should put their house in order before reaching out to the global community and expecting better understanding and global coexistence.

The Saudi Minister of Culture and Information, Abdul Aziz Khoja, who chaired the meeting of the GCC ministers, stated that Gulf States are ready to enhance people-to-people exchanges and cultural cooperation with the outside world. "The culture in the GCC states is based essentially on two great sources: Islam and Arab heritage that advocate tolerance and openness to others," he said.

The decision to enhance cultural cooperation with the outside world is timely with Islamophobia on the rise and Western misconceptions unchecked. Cultural exchange can play a very important role in building bridges of understanding. Enhancing people to people exchanges can also foster friendly relations and better understanding between different cultures.

However, to achieve our desired goals, opinion leaders stress the need for new policies to maintain outreach programs that could reverse the negative attitude toward the both the Gulf countries and Muslims. Policy makers must show more support for global organizations that acknowledge Muslim contributions and exhibit genuine goodwill towards Islam and Muslims.

On the sidelines of the meeting, the GCC ministers honored 18 talented creative artists and popular cultural figures who have promoted the culture and heritage in the Gulf States. We need to recognize more talented young men and women in the Gulf who could participate in international programs and activities to showcase their capabilities and willingness to contribute and develop a peaceful and prosperous world for all people of different nations, faiths and ethnicities

Meanwhile one of the most positive initiatives to support people-to-people cooperation is the global coalition of educators, writers and publishers who come together to confront the continuous acts of defamation of Islam and the smear campaign orchestrated against our heritage and people.

The GCC countries cannot ignore their commitment to recognize the great potential of professional women and to explore new cultural and business opportunities between women in the Gulf and other cultures to promote our heritage and portray a more accurate picture of the Gulf. The participation ofGulf professional women in such initiatives can greatly contribute towards erasing negative stereotypes.

There are also Muslim organizations in the West that deserve more support from Gulf governments to monitor publications, films, cartoons and other damaging stereotypes that propagate hatred and contempt against Islam in Europe and the US. They advocate an end to hostilities and the elimination of the tensions and suspicions that are ruining relations between the Muslim world and the West.

More prominence and support should be provided for global religious leaders who are seeking common grounds and are keen to build trust and respect among all religions.

Media analysts in the Gulf are calling for better plans to put an end to the cycle of suspicion and discord based on false accusations and distorted information to defame our culture and Muslim identity. The GCC should consider a more efficient media strategy and more effective outreach programs with partners in America who are now genuine in their efforts to build bridges of understanding and eager to put an end to the demonization of Islam and Muslims in the United States.

Gulf countries need to establish joint projects between faith-based organizations in order to foster better relations between Muslim communities and the West. The interfaith dialogue initiated by King Abdullah needs to be given better attention by the GCC. More efforts need to be exerted to reach out to faith-based organizations to address the challenges of the 21st century.

It is reaching out to the whole world to promote global prosperity. Let us hope that peaceful partners and allies — as well as religious leaders — will continue to hold on to a spirit of goodwill and mutual respect in order to regain the peace of the world and a better future for our younger generation.

Business Investments Promote Cultural Understanding

The business event "Opportunity Arabia 9" that was held in London on Oct. 1, 2012, was a most welcomed initiative after the blasphemous film against the Prophet Muhammad triggered strong Muslim objections throughout the Middle East and the Muslim world.

It was a refreshing development that offered strong testimonies from leading British personalities and former diplomats dispelling the misconceptions that have created a negative picture of the country and have dissuaded many British companies from investing in Saudi Arabia.

The main objective of the one-day seminar, organized by the Middle East Association (MEA) in partnership with the Committee of International trade of the Saudi Chambers of Commerce, was to foster better trade relations and to project the available business opportunities in Saudi Arabia to the British Business community. The event attracted more than 300 organizations from across British business and industrial sectors.

Sir Alan Monroe, a former ambassador to Saudi Arabia, chaired the meeting. His close business and political connections with Saudi Arabia enriched the presentations with valuable analysis and meaningful commentary.

Distinguished speakers delivered a wealth of information to encourage British investment. They outlined the huge business potentials in infrastructure and the industrial sector and presented serious studies of the growing importance of alternative energy sources to create a healthy environment and a program for more sustainable development in Saudi Arabia. The experts also spoke about the accelerating reforms and the process of modernizing the Kingdom, which is gaining momentum politically, socially and economically.

Sir Sherard Cowper-Coles, chairman of the Saudi British Society and former Ambassador to Saudi Arabia, spoke from the heart when he described Saudi Arabia as the region's richest, most rewarding and lucrative market. He advised those who want to establish fruitful business relationships with the Kingdom to offer quality products and to be willing to share intellectual property and to create genuine joint ventures that would not only take profits but also build blocks of future prosperity.

Omar Bahlaiwa, Secretary General of the Council of Saudi Chambers of Commerce and the Committee of International Trade, presented an informative report about the strength of the Saudi economy and the major investment opportunities in Saudi Arabia.

116

The chairman of the British Business Association in the Kingdom'sEastern Province highlighted the large-scale petrochemical facilities based there and provided necessary information for British investors in petrochemicals fields. Senior British businessmen currently working for Saudi companies in the Kingdom provided advice and valuable data on a wide range of industrial and service sectors

The Business Forum also provided the business community in Britain with briefings, networking opportunities and consultancy advice to encourage British investors to support the implementation of the large-scale development projects in Saudi Arabia. Thamer Jan, the general manager of Commercial Banking at the Saudi British Bank, gave a lengthy presentation about the Saudi economy and the potentials of Saudi businesses partnerships. Basil Ghalayini, CEO of BMG financial group, focused on the major business opportunities available in the infrastructure and the large investment opportunities in the housing sector. The great potential of Saudi women in the workforce was also highlighted, and the British businessmen were introduced to a more positive picture of exceptional Saudi women who are seeking international partners and are keen to promote better trade relations and achieve global prosperity.

The large turnout of British businessmen at the Opportunity Arabia 9 event is an indication that the negative campaign orchestrated against Islam and Saudi Arabia will not succeed. Islamophobia and the defamation of Muslims will not make the country less significant, and it will not affect its political weight as the center of the Muslim world and the world's largest oil producing country. In the midst of the unfortunate East and West turmoil the continued support for similar initiatives by the political and economic establishment can further strengthen bilateral relations and create a better appreciation of differing viewpoints.

The Committee of International Trade is dedicated to promote better trade relations and to create better understanding between Saudi Arabia and the global community.

Interfaith Dialogue Promoting Universal Principles of Tolerance

In the past many conflicts and wars were instigated by religions. Today extremists in all religions are still a threat to humanity and world peace.

At present in Europe, the debate between atheists and believers has also become more bitter and rancorous. However, in spite of the obstructionists, the majority of people in the world still believes in God and consider their faith very necessary and a consoling factor in their daily lives.

Meanwhile, governments are also finally beginning to recognize the important role of religious leaders, who have been marginalized for a long time, in the promotion of peace and global coexistence.

On Nov. 26, the United Nations officially recognized The King Abdullah International Center for Interreligious and Intercultural Dialogue (KAICIID) in Vienna as an international organization that aims to contribute to conflict prevention and resolution, the creation of lasting peace, building bridges between conflicting religions and the promotion of mutual respect and understanding among followers of different religions and cultures. The center includes nearly 800 religious leaders and activists.

There are many controversial issues that religious leaders continue to debate. The Muslim world is greatly concerned with the rise of Islamophobia and the defamation of Islam in the West, while Western religious leaders have been struggling with the concept of separation of church and state.

Atheists and agnostics have called for the removal of the Ten Commandments, the most sacred rules of Christian scripture, and all other things related to Christianity from public property.

The American Civil Liberties Union(ACLU) and its allies as well as other rights groups hostile to religious freedom deny churches the right to rent public school facilities for Sunday worship services. They also deny religious organizations a place in public life, thereby imposing secular life on all of society. Many Christians today remain concerned that a purely secular government that is inherently atheist is dangerously immoral.

Meanwhile, the Sept. 11 attacks and the raging wars and conflicts around the world have made governments and policy makers aware of the urgent need to promote the role of religious leaders who can hopefully bring about peace and global coexistence. The marginalization of religious leaders and the policy of the complete separation of church and state imposed by governments have demonstrated a failure to promote religious values and principles. Faith-based organizations seek to put God back into public life to make the world a more peaceful and moral place.

Religion should not be a source of conflict or division, but rather it should be the means to promote peace and global coexistence. Religious leaders today are encouraged to play a greater role in preaching universal religious principles of tolerance, compassion and justice for all. Faith-based organizations are more vocal in their opposition to those who attempt to use religion to divide all of humanity.

Faith-based organizations continue to criticize politicians who have abused their positions and power. They express concern about the threat of religious extremists who are never held morally accountable for their actions, and they are also disappointed by ineffective religious leaders who have failed to inculcate the correct values that would strengthen the conscience of individuals.

Traditionally, interfaith dialogue groups have been hard to set up, difficult to sustain, and dogged by religious and personal conflicts. However, lately interfaith dialogue initiatives have provided more genuine efforts that are not merely hours of empty rhetoric.

KAICIID will hopefully provide the platform for all the faithful of different religions to rise to the occasion and work together to support interfaith and intercultural organizations as well as change the negative mindset that divides them. Activists and religious scholars are required to seek common ground to confront political, social, economic and environmental issues that are a threat to humanity and world peace.

At the inauguration of KAICIID in Vienna, I met people of different faiths and different beliefs gathered to share their ambition for the creation of a world with no wars and no conflicts — a world with no hatred and violence, and no intercultural tensions and hostilities.

The strong endorsements by the United Nations; the Vatican, which has joined as a founding observer and is represented on the board; and the board of high-level representatives of the major world religions (Judaism, Christianity, Islam, Hinduism and Buddhism) are enough to silence the voices of skeptics and extremists in all religions who are obstacles to peace and a threat to global prosperity.

Father Miguel Angel Ayuso explained: "Dialogue based on respect, mutual understanding and collaboration is a vital necessity for our present and future. As an observer of the Holy See and a member of the Board of Directors for the Catholic Church, I will support the KAICIID in promoting these values."

Ban Ki-moon, the secretary-general of the UN, said, "I fully support your vision of religion as an enabler of respect and reconciliation." He also called on religious leaders to "promote the universal human values and unite under precepts common to all creeds," and he criticized extremist intolerance and the propagators of hate.

The role of religious leaders has become crucial to setting a new direction for the global community. They need to be more effective in order to build trust and eliminate the fears and suspicions that are the reasons behind the turmoil and violence threatening our world today.

Moderation and Peaceful Coexistence

Conflict between different faiths today is caused by deviant viewpoints and misinterpretations of the divine scriptures

To move Saudi Arabia and other Muslim nations forward we need to resolve the ideological crisis that has long-allowed extremely radical views to permeate our societies. The perpetuation of outmoded customs and traditions entwined with Islamic principles need to be untangled to separate the medieval societal customs from the true principles of Islam.

Saudi Arabia has taken major steps to spread the culture of moderation and confront extremism and radicalism that have been permitted to masquerade as the message of Prophet Muhammad (peace be upon Him) and sullied what should be the reputation of faithful Muslims around the world.

Radicalism and extremism, which has spread in Saudi Arabia and some Islamic countries, was fundamentally an ideological crisis. It needed to be addressed more openly and effectively by Muslim scholars and researchers in order to reach a global Muslim consensus that could guide the Muslim nation towards peace and global coexistence. The Saudi leadership on its part has taken major steps in combating extremism and spreading the culture of moderation and tolerance within Saudi society. Many international forums and conferences have been held in the Kingdom to discuss the concept of moderation in Islam and to promote peace and tolerance.

In December 2005, a special Islamic summit was held in Makkah to reaffirm the consensus of all Muslim countries to renounce violence, extremism and terrorism, and to promote values of dialogue, tolerance and mutual respect among religions and cultures.

In May 2008, King Abdullah met Muslim scholars of different sects and ideologies in Makkah to promote the genuine message of Islamic tolerance during the International Islamic Conference for Dialogue.

The Ministry for Islamic Affairs held a series of conferences across the country to combat delinquent thought that is detrimental to the progress and advancement of a Muslim's life in the 21st century.

The Prince Khaled Al-Faisal Chairfor consolidating the Saudi moderation approach was inaugurated at King Abdul Aziz University Jeddah in 2009 with an objective to enable the community to reject the culture of extremism and fanaticism and promote a Saudi moderation approach.

Meanwhile, academics and researchers continue to address the challenges of extremism. During a forum on the concepts of moderation, terrorism and intellectual security, Dr. Abdul Rahman Al-Wahabi, assistant professor at the department of Arabic language at King Abdul Aziz University in Jeddah said that, "discussions about concepts of moderation in contemporary Saudi culture have emerged on a large scale due to the perception of the danger posed by extremist concepts and the prevalence of extremist ideology, particularly in religious thought."

He said activating the process of moderation did not come simply by making wishes, but rather "through intensive educational agendas that are followed by application in real life in an organized manner via a series of social activities."

Zaki Al-Milad an Islamic researcher noted "moderate thought is acknowledgment of others, accepting them and co-existing with them ... moderation should be the attribute that permeates all our ideas and actions, far from radicalism and extremism and far from reclusion and isolationism."

Furthermore, there are concerted efforts to provide direction to Saudi youth that is struggling between two extremes, the religious hardliners and the foreign influences that go against Muslim values and principles. There are summer camps and cultural activities offering guidance and mentoring to promote better citizens who can contribute to humanity and serve the Muslim nation worldwide. The whole country is on a mission to empower an educated and more tolerant generation that can command respect for its spirituality and academic excellence. Academic institutions encourage progressive thinking and allow students to embrace innovative ideas without compromising their Islamic values and principles.

Our brothers and sisters who are living in the West or in other Muslim countries need to be aware that there are moderate Saudi religious scholars and progressive Saudi people under the leadership of King Abdullah who promote moderation and reject extremism. The Kingdom has initiated a national program for intellectual dialogue with extremists and Al-Qaeda sympathizers as a means to rehabilitate them, to contain extremism and spread the culture of moderation and tolerance within society.

Every Muslim today should make it his or her duty to discard the unfounded fears and the growing hostility towards Islam that have lead to the discrimination, stereotyping, and hate crimes against Muslims today. It is about time that ordinary Muslims take responsibility to dispel the lies of Western extremists and speak out against their own extremists who have hijacked the religion and continue to hold distorted interpretations of the Quran and that give Islam a bad name. Every Muslim should also be responsible for correcting the misconceptions about Islam that started with Samuel Huntington's theory of a clash of civilizations and later fueled by suspicious allegations by right-wing outlets and extremists. These extremists are naturally aided by the likes of Daniel Pipes, Steve Emerson, Judith Miller, Bernard Lewis and many others.

The 9/11 attack against the United States compounded the suspicions and fears against Muslims and created extreme prejudices against them. The principle of collective guilt was applied to all Muslims and 10 years after 9/11 a vicious campaign continues to label Islam as monolithic and unable to adapt to new realities, that it is a religion inferior to the West, and that it does not share common values with the other major faiths.

There are those in the West, whose growing hostility toward Islam leads to discrimination and sometimes even hate crimes and who use extremist tactics to drive a wedge between Islam and the West.

There are many global Muslim organizations that are trying hard to confront this unjust attack. However, in spite of all their efforts Islamophobia is on the rise, and Muslims are still stereotyped as inferior, violent and unable to adapt to new realities. The Organization of Islamic Cooperation, the Muslim World League among many other global Muslim organizations continues to address the rise of Islamophobia that openly targets innocent Muslims around the world.

The conflict between different faiths today is caused by deviant viewpoints and misinterpretations of the divine scriptures. Extremists on both sides undermine the noble efforts of the peace loving people of the world. It pains me to hear Muslim extremists attacking the moderates when they speak out against their hard-line views. It also saddens me to listen to the bigotry and hatred against Muslims in the West fomented by extremist Christian preachers who in reality are no less twisted than our own extremists.

The time has now come for all the peace-loving people to unite and stand against radicals who continue to undermine global efforts to promote peace and coexistence. Domestically, we will see the carefully crafted plans of our leaders begin the positive changes they have wanted to bring us for so long. Globally, we will see the beginning of a new era in which each human being — man and woman — can be assured of the respect and freedom that only a just and peaceful world can provide.

Lessons from the Egyptian Revolution.

There are many lessons to be learnt from the Egyptian revolution. What is needed in Egypt and the Arab world today is a new approach of accepting and respecting the differences between all segments in society — Muslims and Copts, liberals and conservatives — to put an end to hostilities and eliminate the tension and divisions that threaten the nation's stability. The Egyptian government must restore calm and order before the country is dragged into a civil war that will have no end.

The Egyptian Revolution continues after the former elected president of Egypt Mohamed Morsi failed to bring calm and end the chaos, violence and unrest that is eroding the social fabric of Egypt's diverse society.

The Egyptian people had great expectations and were hopeful that the election of the first civilian president would usher in a more prosperous future. However, Morsi failed to understand that the Egyptian people elected him as a leader to serve their interests, they did not elect the Muslim Brotherhood to control their lives. He failed in his task to achieve reconciliation between the different groups in society. He did not reach out to the 50 percent of the population who did not vote for him, among them the secular, liberal, and Christian elements in Egyptian society. He was unable to ensure them that their views and aspirations would be honored in a government of religious and political pluralism. His policies did not guarantee that all Egyptians would have an opportunity to contribute or benefit from the progress of their country.

Ousted President Morsi disappointed many Egyptians who hoped for a civil, democratic, constitutional and modern state. Public resentment and mistrust continued with hardly any economic or social progress.

Morsi's government failed to conduct proper restructuring of government departments and was not efficient in appointing qualified staff to implement much needed reforms. Managing and capitalizing on Egyptian human resources is a major task that can guarantee social justice and improve the standard of living of the Egyptian people. The aspirations of the Egyptian public must be met with concrete action by capable individuals rather than by those whose only qualification is that they are supporters of those in control.

The chaos and uncertainty are what prompted tens of thousands of citizens to flock to Tahrir Square to vent their anger and rage at the state of affairs in peaceful disobedience. They will no doubt support any positive change and policies that can provide them with a life of dignity and self-respect. Political analysts assert that the immediate challenge is restoring stability and enforcing law and order. There is an urgent need to establish a more effective police force to end the state of lawlessness and to enhance professional police performance to protect the innocent. Morsi failed to serve justice according to the international standards of human rights. Egypt today is in dire need of trust between government and civil institutions that represent public interests and demands. There are still many challenges facing this new people's revolution and there are no clear and certain solutions.

The media must act in a more responsible way to voice people's concerns and frustrations. It should play a more active role in creating a spirit of solidarity between the different factions of Egyptian society to help them achieve their national goal of building a democratic country rather than driving them apart by inflammatory talk shows and publications with accusations that cause further divisions and mistrust.

Any future government should not underestimate the aspirations of the people who represent a strong force that demands transparency. Egyptian youth feel that their demands for justice and equal opportunities have not been met, so they continue to protest for better policies that serve their interests and address their concerns. They are a generation that can no longer be subservient to dictators and unqualified leaders. The youth have created a large network to expose human rights violations. They will continue to do so until new government officials address urgent social, economic and political challenges.

Egyptian women have shown courage and have also played an important role in the Egyptian revolt. They boldly participated in the Tahrir Square protests. Women online activists were instrumental in exposing government excesses nationwide. The new government should make sure that qualified women are given the opportunity to have a say in government and a future role in building their nation.

Human rights and freedom of speech are the order of the day. Policy makers today cannot get away with false promises and cosmetic changes. Governments can only succeed if they build trust and implement laws that provide justice for all. Public discontent should be addressed with immediate efforts to serve the common man rather than merely addressing the needs of the few who are in power.

The whole world is watching the developments of the Egyptian Revolution. People around the world are still inspired by the broadcast of images of patriotic Egyptians determined to save their revolution and striving to fight dictatorship and failed, monolithic governments.

All Arabs and the global community sincerely wish the Egyptian people success; they have the right to choose their leaders and to hope for a prosperous future in which all of their voices will be heard and in which they are able to help guide the ship of state.

Australia Takes a New Stand on Palestine

Australia was among the 41 nations that abstained from a vote on whether the Palestinian territories should be granted observer status at the United Nations, defying US and Israeli pressure to vote against the resolution.

The subject was raised during a meeting with a high-level trade delegation of the Australia Gulf Council, AGC, at the Jeddah Chamber of Commerce and Industry (JCCI). Saudi businessmen expressed their appreciation for Australia's stand and indicated that the Palestinian issue has always been a thorn in the diplomatic and trade relations between Arabs and countries of the West. They added that this new development could progress trade and cultural relations between the Kingdom and Australia.

Australian Foreign Affairs Minister Bob Carr said that Australia is entitled to make foreign policy decisions that are different from America's. He said that the prime minister had shown strong leadership over the issue and that voting no would have indicated that Australia did not support Palestinian statehood in any context.

He also said, "I saw a prime minister engaging with party opinion, listening to what people had to say from all over the nation, and from every corner of Labor Party opinion and doing what good leaders do, and that is speak for the whole party. This vote had become a referendum on the idea of a Palestinian state, and if we'd voted no it would be widely interpreted that we don't support Palestinian statehood.

"A clear majority of countries supported the resolution; however, abstaining put Australia in a different position from Israel, which opposes granting the territories observer status. We're a Labor government, and from time to time we'll have a difference with the United States," Carr said.

Earlier former foreign minister Gareth Evans briefing MPs, remarked that Israel had misread the situation by not recognizing that the best way to shore up the Palestinian National Authority was to support the resolution.

"My very strong view was that to vote no on this resolution would be not to help the cause of peace, not to help Israel and to be putting Australia absolutely on the wrong side of history in terms of our region and in terms of our capacity to be a credible and effective performer on the Security Council over the next two years," he said. "I genuinely believed that this would be a foreign policy catastrophe and one of the worst decisions we could possibly make if we were to go down this particular path. A yes vote or an abstention vote were equally acceptable and would be equally understood internationally. It's a no vote that would have created huge problems for us."

The Australian stand on the Palestine issue at the UN is a first step in recognizing that the Palestinian issue is part of Australia's foreign policy. Arab sources and political analysts believe that by adopting this position Australia can play a more positive role in Middle East negotiations.

There are no standing issues between Australia and the Arab world and the GCC countries in particular. On the contrary both sides can gain from each other through trade, finance and cultural cooperation.

The AGC business delegation, led by Mark Vaile, former deputy prime minister of Australia and former minister for trade, included Anna Bligh, former Queensland premier, and Ahmed Fahour, the Australian special envoy to the Organization of Islamic Cooperation (OIC).

Bligh said she believes there is huge potential for improving business and commercial ties between Australian businesses and Saudi entrepreneurs. She said that there are approximately 12,000 Saudi students studying in Australian universities and about 72,000 family members are accompanying them.She hoped that research partnership and business relations would strengthen further in decades to come. She pointed out that prayer rooms have been included in Australian shopping malls and that Queensland often has signs in Arabic to welcome visitors.

Fahour said Saudi citizens could obtain visitor visas to Australia online within 48 hours. "We have provided this facility exclusively for Saudis under a special initiative," he said, adding that applying online to obtain visas to Australia had become fast since it could be done from home and work.

Jonathan Herps, chief executive officer of the AGC, highlighted the objective of the AGC to facilitate increased two-way trade and investment by representing Australia's corporate partners and GCC countries at the highest level. Australia's two-way merchandise trade with Saudi Arabia has risen to 2.15 billion Australian dollars with major exports in 2011-12 including passenger motor vehicles, barley, wheat and meat.

The business mission included chief and senior executives from automotive, agriculture, construction and engineering, education, financial services, food and beverage, transport, telecommunications and tourism.

"We are all looking forward to building new opportunities to create new partnerships that will continue to foster our connections with this region," Fahour said.He added that in order to create strong business links we need strong people-to-people links. On that basis we are saying that Australia will build an Islamic museum, which will be opening next year. It has good support from Saudi-based institutions, one of them being the Organization of Islamic Cooperation (OIC) based in Jeddah, he said.

The AGC works closely with the Australian government and in particular the Department of Foreign Affairs and Trade (DFAT) and Austrade, which have been crucial in the establishment and operation of the AGC. The AGC also works with Australian state government representatives in GCC countries.

Chapter 8

THE MEDIA

- Media Adopts Women's Causes
- Saudi Media and Civil Society
- Online Journalism
- Social Media a Major Force in SA
- Young Journalists Engines for Change

Media Adopts Women's Causes

Saudi journalists have engaged Islamic scholars and encouraged public debate to articulate Islam's position on women to lead society on the right track. Opinion leaders portray scientific, moderate Islamic and international trends that honor women and respect their rights that enables them to become engines for change and pave the way for activists and civil society to revise women's marginalized status.

The Saudi media has on several occasions adopted the causes of women who suffer from discrimination and given them wide publicity Of particular note are the cases of Rania Al-Baz, the famous TV personality who was badly beaten up by her husband; Fatima and Mansour Al-Timani who were forced to separate because of tribal discrimination; the Qatif girl who was raped but did not find justice; Yara who was arrested for meeting a colleague for business at a Starbucks Café; Manal Alshereef who was arrested for daring to drive in the Eastern Province and many other cases of social injustice and domestic abuse. The newspapers have also reported the opinions of human-rights advocates who were critical of prison conditions, exaggerated jail terms and flogging of women.

More importantly, the papers continue to campaign for a codified system to reprimand judges who build cases against women without Shariah guidelines. A structured justice system would ensure a uniform application of Sharia law.

The opinion pages in the local press are very critical of the controversial interpretations of some judges and have exposed injustices in cases of child marriages, sexual abuse, child custody and divorce on grounds of social or racial status. Eloquent columnists have been very effective in urging decision makers to confront current challenges and accelerate reforms. They continue to push for new laws and regulations that could ease the integration of women into the work force in areas such as driving, maternity leave, working hours, on-site nurseries and equal pay.

The English language newspapers have also played an important role. The fact that they are published in an Arab country has not made them less supportive of women's issues; on the contrary, their coverage is even more effective than some of the Arabic dailies in exposing the mistakes against women. The excellent opinion pieces and eloquent analyses of women's needs and concerns advance change in the mindsets of many who once resisted change and insisted that women should remain inside their homes and on the sidelines of our economy. Among the most prominent and successful campaigns that encouraged the participation of women was the Arab News Top 20 Businesswomen list which was a very powerful endorsement of the existing companies that are successfully run by women.

Local newspapers continue to carry many bold articles calling for new policies to eliminate extremist religious practices that oppose the modernization of Saudi society, including the opposition to women driving; the reluctance to vote for women in the chambers of commerce elections; the strict culture of segregation within the society; the niqab, which compromises the level of efficiency and professionalism of women's careers; discrimination policies at the workplace; and underestimating women's business abilities.

Women's magazines such as Sayidity, Laha, the Arabian Woman and others havebeen very effective in their successful campaigns to include women in the decision-making process.They campaigned enthusiastically for the inclusion of women in the Shoura Council and lifting the ban on women standing for municipal elections.

None deny that the road to progress will be difficult and that women have a long way to go to achieve their desired goals. However, with the support of dedicated reporters and opinion leaders they can hope to overcome the many challenges that exist. Saudi media has projected many young and talented women who are determined to modernize their country and fulfil their dreams and aspirations.

Social media and civil society

There is a new breed of young Saudis who are the products of the Internet age and are well aware of the powers of citizen journalism. They are outspoken, and they openly express their opinions in blogs Twitter and Facebook. The Internet has exposed them to more advanced communities, and they are not willing to follow blindly the footsteps of their fathers whose silence allowed corruption to creep into their society and permitted injustices to continue without any checks.

The upsurge in social media began with the flooding of the city of Jeddah on Dec. 29, 2009. Young activists mourned the city of Jeddah on Facebook and twitter in 2009 and demonstrated their rage and utter frustration over the corruption, reckless attitude and indifference of government officials and public servants who were responsible for an unforgivable tragedy of death, destruction and ruin.

Young bloggers were angry over the failure of officials to build a proper infrastructure for the city of Jeddah. They criticized the government's neglect of urban planning, which brought out this calamity. They discussed the looming threats that were presented again and again by environmentalists, researchers and businessmen, and shared the reports that were deliberately ignored and the extensive research that warned of the disaster. Social media circulated the story of Jeddah's anger over the inability of government departments to provide swift and professional help that could have minimized the loss of lives and curbed the devastating destruction of homes and property.

King Abdullah's compassionate address to the city of Jeddah and his promise to punish those responsible, his million-riyal compensation to the families of the dead, and the provision of homes for the displaced families have somewhat calmed the rage of the residents and provided some solace to many. The King ordered the immediate formation of a commission of inquiry to investigate and announce its findings of where things went wrong and who was to blame.

Media professionals, concerned citizens, activists and young volunteers held an emergency meeting to devise a strategy in order to confront the dangerous situation and bring calm and awareness to the frightened and devastated victims. In a heated discussion, representatives of each group vowed never to allow this manmade tragedy to happen again. The young volunteers who witnessed the death and destruction were very outspoken and wary of the policy of their elders who were passive in dealing with their problems and concerns. Their angry voices criticized the lack of accountability and the mismanagement of government resources.

Blogs and Tweets voiced their concerns and initiated a campaign of search-and-rescue operations, they brought to public notice the heroic acts of individuals who lost their lives to save the drowning and ease the hardships of the devastated victims who were living in ruins.

Social media was also engaged in keeping the public aware of the existing dangers and provided accurate information with pictures and live images of the destroyed districts. It exposed the inefficiency of government departments, the inadequate equipment and the unavailability of expertise that could have offered logistical and necessary professional support.

This tragedy has revealed the glaring incompetence, negligence, and lack of expertise among officials and public servants. There are obvious reasons behind this, including the absence of monitoring bodies to supervise the implementation of government reforms and services and the lack of a supervisory committee to monitor the conduct of people in public office. This situation has made it more imperative for the media and civil society to play the watchdog role in order to protect human rights and root out the corruption that runs deep in some government departments, organizations and public institutions.

Social activists today feel optimistic over the level of awareness and courage among the younger population. They believe that the lesson from this tragedy could teach citizens to become more critical of the misconduct of government officials and expose their corruption and deceit. Social activists have intensified their efforts to create public awareness, protect human rights and address the needs of society in a more scientific and professional manner. Many believe that good might come out of this disaster. They are of the opinion that only such a tragedy could have triggered the vitally urgent reforms. There are pressing demands for better policies that can serve the interests of society and guarantee a life of dignity and prosperity for all citizens

The government has begun to recognize the need for increased numbers of qualified experts who can provide global standards to implement reforms. It has been embarrassed before the world by the apparent negligence of some decision-makers who allowed this tragedy to take place. It is certainly unacceptable for a country of the international economic stature of Saudi Arabia with its abundant resources to allow this kind of injustice to be inflicted upon its people.

Social Media a Major Force in Saudi Arabia.

Researchers at the Dubai School of Government released a study recently on social media in the Arab world. According to the report, Saudis are the most active social media users in the Arab region, with an estimated 393,000 using Twitter and nearly four million using Facebook.

In Saudi Arabia the rapid rise of social media has increased civic awareness and youth engagement in public affairs, and its popularity has introduced new social dynamics. It has become an essential tool in the lives of many people and has emerged as one of the main methods of networking and social interaction between individuals, businesses and government.

Young Saudis today debate all sorts of issues on social media and use it as a tool to enable their voices to reach officials and to network and connect with people who share their interests and activities. They are not afraid to express their frustrations and to criticize officials or the negative behavior and attitudes of ultraconservatives in society who do not support change and modernity.

Citizen journalism has gained popularity, and young people have become more eager to voice their opinions and to influence change for a better future. They no longer tolerate being led by the incompetent or the hardliners who are insensitive to their needs and concerns.

The increasing number of young activists on Twitter, Facebook and YouTube is an indication that young people will become both more active and involved in public affairs. Their level of awareness will make it very difficult for government not to strive harder to remove corruption and the obstacles standing in the way of progress.

The conflict between the progressives and the hardliners in society is more prominent online and among social media users. A more healthy, peaceful and constructive national debate needs to be encouraged online and in the print media in order to create harmony and unity among all citizens.

People involved in social media have a responsibility to encourage an objective debate that can contribute to the welfare of the country. The hardline position of some elders and the inability to accept criticism is a dangerous phenomenon. Some officials only pay lip service to young people's demands, and they trivialize their interaction with young minds. The social media, apart from the occasional official and sometimes sites, is the voice of the people and media professionals need to keep up their campaign to influence change and support social cohesion. It has taken the watchdog role to protect the interests of all citizens.

The social media in the Arab worldhas been instrumental in rallying people around social causes and political campaigns, boosting citizen journalism and civic participation, creating a forum for debate and interaction between the government and the society.However, in Saudi Arabia social media tools have been exploited and are often viewed negatively and with suspicion. Many fail to recognize the contributions of social media toward unity, social harmony and economic growth.

The leading social media agency in the Middle East, the Dubai School of Government, in its 2012 report on Arab social media lays emphasis on the potential for increasing,collaboration, knowledge sharing and innovation, both between and among government entities, citizens and the private sector. Social networking businesses have become an important asset for the most successful companies; they connect more than 550 million people globally and provide an infrastructure for thousands of start-ups and social entrepreneurs. It would be more constructive to explore the creative potential of social media to build diverse businesses and services rather than to undermine or censure its contributions to its large and increasing audience.

Bloggers and Facebook users have become more outspoken in criticizing the policies that affect their lives and the progress of their country. Others will not give up their right to tweet their criticism of policies that affect their lives or the negligence of officials who are responsible for social or economic problems.

Censorship and suppression belong to the past. Young people today demand to be heard, and they will not give up their right to express their opinion without political or social restrictions It is critical at this stage to encourage a more objective and constructive national debate within social media and to engage the younger generation positively. It is equally important to recognize the increasing power of social media and its capacity to mobilize thousands of citizen journalists at any given time. Above all it is very important not to underestimate the influence of social media at home and around the world.

Online Journalism in the Gulf

The future of online writers and journalism in the Gulf is very uncertain. Current methods of generating online revenue cannot offset the loss of the traditional advertising that mainstream printed and tele-visual media relies upon to sustain their businesses.

In order to survive, mainstream media must come up with innovative ideas to upgrade their information services and to compete with the emerging technologies of online media. Gulf online writers, journalists and media professionals from Malaysia, Eastern Europe and the United States took part in a workshop organized by the International Research and Exchanges

Board,(IREX) to address these challenges and discuss the current situation in the Gulf.

The participants included young, talented bloggers who represented the popular new trend of citizen journalism. They debated the role of new forms of media that are changing and reshaping public debate.

Case studies from Kuwait, Bahrain and Saudi Arabia demonstrated the growing popularity of blogs and online forums and allowed the bloggers to express their views and frustrations over being constantly threatened with shutdown, and in some cases prison terms, for simply providing people with an online forum to discuss their demands for change and other issues of public interest.

The young bloggers rejected any forms of control on free speech and maintained that as amateur bloggers they are entitled to express personal opinions and should not be expected to conform to standards and rules imposed on professional journalists.

In a session that examined the relationship between citizen journalists, bloggers and mainstream media, media professionals highlighted the efforts of mainstream media to adopt the new information technologies in order to keep pace with the ever-changing information revolution.

Online editors shared experiences of employing electronic news sources and creating online relationships with readers. IT experts and media professionals gave an impressive presentation outlining the emerging technologies for online media. They demonstrated how Web 2.0 changed the media landscape and discussed methods to integrate multimedia into existing content.

It was evident that media companies must balance needed investments in technology and content with dwindling revenue resources. Participants discussed the new era of citizen journalism that has created a more vibrant sociopolitical debate. Bloggers opposed alliances with traditional media, preferring independence to criticize social and political issues and expose corruption and human rights violations.

Young bloggers criticized Arab mainstream media and rejected the idea of conforming to official journalist association rules and guidelines. They insisted on maintaining both their independence and their freedom to express their opinions to help shape the public debate. In a heated discussion about ethics for online journalism, bloggers refused to conform to any code of ethics, and they did not want to be labeled professional journalists and vehemently asserted their right to express their opinions in any form without any ethical, political, social or literary restriction. They openly criticized the Arab mainstream media for its lack of professionalism and failure to expose corruption and provide more accurate reports on issues that affect everyday lives of the people.

The participants discussed the impact of blogging in Gulf countries. Kuwaiti blogger Abdul Aziz Al Ateeqi said blogs had become a key part of the political process in Kuwait. Issues they had tackled evolved from local community and social issues to news, political scandals, and corruption. In Kuwait, the *Bas* (Enough) campaign succeeded in supporting women's suffrage in 2005, and in changing the electoral system in 2006.

Omani blogger Muawiyah Al Rawahi said online discussions allow individuals to tackle issues that news outlets do not cover well in order not to offend government officials. Tawfeeq Al Rayyash, a Bahraini blogger said if the government blocks some popular sites or discussion forums and imposes restrictions, they can always find ways around those restrictions, using proxy sites and other methods to maneuver around government controls.

Panelist Evgeny Morozov, author of Foreign Policy magazine's "Net Effects" column, said, "people will continue blogging no matter what laws or ethical regulations we're going to impose (they are) simply not going to be enforceable."

Conversely, mainstream editors and journalists were critical of the unethical behavior of many bloggers and asserted that bloggers should be held accountable for spreading inaccurate information and face libel and defamation prosecutions if they did not conform to information laws.

Jamal Khashoggi, the former editor of the Saudi Arabian Al-Watan newspaper ,argued that the contents of blogs and online forums should be monitored and regulated to protect the public interest. He stressed the importance of applying standards for verifying the credibility and accuracy of sources and conclusions.

Amer al Hilaliya, a Kuwaiti blogger and journalist, criticized Arab journalism that is based almost solely on opinion with hardly any investigative reporting. He also said he saw more investigative reporting in the Arab blogosphere than in mainstream Arab media.

One of the highlights of the workshop was a commentary by Katharine Zaleski, senior editor for special projects for the online magazine Huffington Post, who shared the experience of the popular Internet newspaper and outlined the site's impact on the broader media community during the 2008 US elections and demonstrated how citizens supported the Obama campaign electronically. The Huffington Post represents a futuristic model of leadership in citizen journalism, mobilizing hundreds of citizen journalists to report on the 2008 elections through its "Off the Bus" program.

The site recently announced it intended to launch the Huffington Post Investigative Fund that would fund 10 staff journalists to work exclusively on investigative reporting. The Huffington Post won the 2006 and 2008 Webby Awards for the Best Political Blog and was recently named one of the Top 25 blogs by Time Magazine. Firsthand information on the latest developments in the field and the progress of online American newspapers was very valuable.

The workshop on online writers and journalism in the Gulf also provided an opportunity for young bloggers to network and exchange views with editors of mainstream media.

The Bloggers from Kuwait, Bahrain and Saudi Arabia were eager to learn and adopt new forms of media technologies to influence change and instigate reforms. Online editors and journalists recognized that citizen journalists could help them upgrade information services and provide better news content.

In the final session of the workshop and after a long, heated discussion, participants concluded that only time will tell how the information technologies will develop and what the future holds for bloggers and mainstream media. The important question remains: Will citizen journalism in the Gulf succeed in serving the public interest?

Young Saudis today debate all sorts of issues online and use it as a tool to have their voices reach officials and to network and connect with people who share their interests and activities. They are not afraid to express their frustrations and criticize officials or the negative behavior and attitudes of the ultra conservatives who do not support change and modernity.

Citizen journalism has gained popularity, and young people have become more eager to voice their opinions and influence change towards a better future. They can no longer tolerate being led by the incompetent or the hardliners who are insensitive to their needs and concerns.

The increasing number of young activists on Twitter, Facebook and YouTube is an indication that young people will become more active and more involved in public affairs. Their level of awareness will make it very difficult for governments not to strive harder to remove corruption and the obstacles standing in the way of progress.

The conflict between the progressive and the hardliners is more prominent online and among social media users. A more healthy, peaceful and constructive national debate needs to be encouraged online and in print media in order to create harmony and unity among all citizens.

People involved in social media have a responsibility to encourage an objective debate that can contribute towards the welfare of the country. The hard-line position of the elders and their inability to accept criticism is a dangerous phenomenon. Officials pay lip service to young people's demands and they trivialize their interaction with the young minds. Meanwhile media professionals have not played an effective role to support social cohesion and have taken a mild stand in voicing public opinion.

The Role of Young Journalists

Print media has taken a secondary position, and most newspapers and magazines have created an online interactive service to attract the attention of the young generation that prefers to read the news online. However, the power of the media remains strong in whatever form, albeit social media, online or print media.

In Saudi Arabia young people are becoming more involved in the media services to create a better tomorrow for Saudi citizens. Among the most talented are a group of young men and women who have established their own publishing houses in order to serve the more educated young professionals and to make a difference in society.

The founders and editors of two Saudi English language magazines, Dazzle and What's Up, Jeddah? have made an impact among educated and progressive young Saudis. These young men and women play a role in preserving their heritage and culture while providing their readers with what is progressive and global. Dazzle and What's Up are monthly magazines, focused on projecting everything Saudi to the rest of the world.

The young media professionals represent a new image of Saudis who are progressive in their outlook and conservative in their behavior, very keen to stay in touch with their roots but at the same time promoting new trends to serve their community. The young journalists are determined to provide a better way of life that could help members of society compete with the global and more advanced countries of the world today.

Reham Abul wafa ,Ghadeer Zainy and Danya Alsafadi, the co-owners of Dazzle, feature focused articles that address the challenges facing the 21st century professional Saudi woman. Supported by a staff of 10 talented women writers, editors, web designers and IT specialists, they provide the latest reports and research related to women's health, psychology and family affairs, and scientific analysis from a Saudi perspective. The articles address the challenges facing women and the opportunities available to empower and help them succeed.

The all-woman Dazzle team believes in the need to encourage new trends that can serve the new sophisticated and professional young women living in Saudi Arabia. The women's magazine projects the work and talents of women who have something unique to offer to society. It serves the trendsetters who wish to promote their brands, featuring the latest collections of aspiring fashion designers who have introduced colorful hijabs and stylish robes to cater to the majority of women un able to find suitable clothes in the market today, or new trends in designs that are inspired by the local culture and is more Arabic in décor and Islamic in architecture.

The young professional journalists are on a mission to discover successful stories of Saudi women who were able to persevere and achieve their goals without compromising their role as mothers or their Muslim identity. Dazzle has become widespread, and it now has a global reach that projects this new image of the educated professional women in business, banking, doctors, fashion and interior designers and other professionals who have been integrated into the Saudi workforce today.

What's Up Jeddah? is another magazine with a mission to serve young Saudis and promote the Saudi culture and lifestyle. Brothers Ghaith and Ghassan Alabdali and Turki Bin Abdullah founded it in 2005. The three young men studied in the UK and came back to contribute towards the development of their society. During the past seven years they have gained popularity and featured many articles promoting young community leaders and trendsetters. The magazine caters to young professionals and entrepreneurs and provides updated information about the products and the services of leading companies. The monthlylifestyle magazine is also focused on providing the latest in fashion trends, designs, electronics, business, travel, autos, as well as food and restaurants. It is distributed in Jeddah and

Riyadh, and covers the latest events and activities that are popular among the youth today.

Media and literary contributions among the younger population are an indication of the development of the thought process within society. Only in societies where free flow of thoughts and ideas occur will social development take place. Communities bloom when there are diverse opinions. We need to recognize the value of specialized magazines as they occupy an important niche that affects the cultural and economic maturity. Young Saudi journalists today have an important role to play in the challenging process of modernizing Saudi Arabia.

Chapter 9

Civil Activism

- Civil Activism Driving Reform
- A Catalyst for Social Change
- A Coalition of Civil Society
- Saudi Research Centers Promote Development
- Addressing Social Ills
- Raising Public Awareness of Health Issues
- The Role of Business
- Antiquated Laws and Regulations
- Codified Shariah Laws

Civil Activism Driving Reform

Prince Sultan University – Girls' College and in cooperation with the UNDP Regional Program for Capacity Building in the Arab States, held the first workshop in 2007 on Young Women Leaders in the Arab Region with an objective to develop the leadership skills for young women.

The workshop aimed at training 150 Saudi young women to enhance their leadership skills and enable them to establish a community of practice on leadership issues.

The women's section of the Saudi Human Rights Commission also held a three-day workshop in December 2010 with Prince Sultan University's School of Law to promote the concept of human rights in society and to outline the related international human rights agreements to which Saudi Arabia is a signatory.

The presentations focused on raising the awareness of women to enable them to use the legal system to file complaints, highlighting that many incidences of domestic abuse go unreported due to fear.

The Human Rights Commission has been active in monitoring the implementation of rules and regulations and has taken action against many issues that violate the legitimate rights and civil liberties of Saudi citizens, investigating domestic violence and promoting women's rights and children's rights, inspecting prison conditions and advocating prisoners rights.

Reformers and social activists are working hard to serve justice and the interests of abused women and children. Media and social media campaigns continue to openly criticize the hard line mentality that is so resistant to change.

Catalyst for Social Change

Princess **Ameerah Al-Taweel** was an eloquent participant in the Clinton Global Imitative panel discussion moderated by**Piers Morgan in 2012 in New York. She spoke about Saudi reforms and the work of** Alwaleed Bin Talal Foundation as an NGO organization to influence change and facilitate reforms.

The Princess stressed the importance of building civil society and local non-governmental organizations (NGOs) as the two main factors that could contribute to the development of Saudi Arabia.

I could not agree more with the Princess; a strong and vibrant civil society strengthens responsible citizenship and supports government work. NGOs today address issues in support of the public good; they perform a variety of services and humanitarian functions, to bring public concerns to governments, monitor policy and program implementation and encourage participation of civil society stakeholders at the community level.

NGOs deliver services such as loans, job training, educational assistance, and community development to the public to support government services.

Global communications have greatly influenced civil society in the Arab and Muslim world. They have inspired the average citizen to know or care enough to participate in political life. More and more citizens are becoming well informed and are shaping public choices.

In the Arab world, civic organizations, particularly NGOs, have multiplied in the past decade. In Egypt alone there are roughly 14,000 registered NGOs, the existence of which has contributed to the empowerment of its citizens. Civic organizations provided forums for citizens to pursue shared interests, both political and social, collectively and peacefully.

Egyptian activists used civic organizations to mobilize millions of citizens against the repressive regime to introduce a democratic alternative to the status quo.

International human rights organizations and the pro-democracy movements encouraged the formation of Arab human rights and democracy organizations. Foreign aid and support for NGOs encouraged the growth of civic groups.

In Saudi Arabia and the Gulf countries however the majority of the civic organizations and associations, support the status quo, and advocate conservative reforms, or are simply apolitical. In the past few years many NGOs have been set up under government directives. Nonprofit organizations, religious organizations, business associations, societies, charity organizations, and research institutions are some of the civic organizations that are striving to empower Gulf citizens.

However, civil society is being hindered by legal structures that do not allow the formation of civil institutions and non-governmental organizations. Currently the law requires all welfare societies to register under the central authority umbrella and highly restrictive procedures are imposed to ban the activities of civil society groups eager to address issues of social concern such as labor rights or gender equality. They are closely monitored and regulated to prevent financial and administrative abuse, yet the bureaucratic procedures and the legal and regulatory frameworks that govern their establishment are detrimental to their efforts to contribute in public life. Moreover, among the reasons for the inability of Saudi NGOs to bring sustainable impact has been their failure to connect with the larger sociopolitical systems and the surrounding institutional structures

In the past, civil society activities were confined to *diwaniyyas*, which are regular private gatherings of relatives, friends, and colleagues that serve as forums for, conducting business and discussing social concerns.

However, Saudi Arabia and the Gulf countries are finally witnessing a new era, and a vibrant civil society is emerging. Young people and social media are supporting the NGO movement by putting pressure on governments to be accountable, to implement the rule of law, and to apply international standards of good government.

The rule of law helps build a healthy society that recognizes civil and political rights, which include freedom of expression and participation in public affairs. Civil society acts as a watchdog to safeguard the interests of the public and the government. Today Gulf citizens, whether rich or poor, are well aware of their right to hold their government accountable. What they need is the capacity to do so.

Developing countries in the Gulf need the expertise of the more advanced countries to formulate the legal and regulatory framework that can facilitate civic participation in public affairs. Building the capacity of civic groups is essential for sustainability of future investments.

Good governance depends on the existence of both a strong state and a healthy and active civil society. In order to build a more vibrant civil society in the Gulf we need to train and support citizens to learn how to Identify their problems and develop a mechanism to serve their community.

Civil society movements represent citizen interests; they are the necessary means to assist in shaping both government policy and social attitudes.

A Coalition of Civil Society

A coalition of civic organizations can work toward applying an inclusive problem-solving approach and help develop more adequate strategies to implement reforms. Government alone cannot satisfy the requirements of the market.

The Council of Ministers recently approved the establishment of a high-level committee, chaired by Labor Minister Adel Fakeih, to oversee the Saudization of operation and maintenance jobs in government departments. It will be required to activate royal decrees, implement related resolutions and present an annual report to higher authorities explaining its achievements and difficulties

Hopefully this committee will make a difference and can come up with better plans to boost Saudization efforts.

The business community continues to be wary of the Saudization strategy, and those seeking employment are frustrated over their inability to qualify for market needs.

Despite the many programs initiated by the Ministry of Labor to upgrade the skills of Saudi citizens and the large budget allocated to the Ministry of Education to raise the quality of education, many of our young graduates entering the workforce are still unqualified. Moreover, the government so far cannot accommodate the large numbers of unskilled laborers, and the private sector is not willing to lose its businesses to accommodate them. The Nitaqat initiative has not succeeded in addressing the creation of sufficient new jobs for the unemployed and has not provided the proper environment for them to contribute to the nation building.

The government continues to be challenged to revise the Saudization strategy, amend laws and regulations, supervise and monitor a more efficient implementation of new regulations and initiatives.

It would be tragic if we compromise on international standards of safety in operations and maintenance jobs. The public needs a commitment to rejuvenate public services with changes in managerial and maintenance personnel. Incompetent officials should be replaced with more creative, qualified experts who could provide more innovative strategies for administrative services, operations, emergency rules, maintenance and technical work, all of which are vital elements in the maintenance of international standards of services rendered to citizens.

The Kingdom's industries are disappointed over the poor skill level and technical acumen despite the amount of revenue being spent to upgrade government maintenance and operation sectors. Maintenance and operations are serious tasks that require thorough training and education to produce qualified skilled laborwith the appropriate mind-set. More people should be encouraged to take on maintenance and technical jobs, and the negative attitude towards them should be corrected. The public must recognize that the services of technical personnel and skilled laborers are vital to our national economy.

Saudi Airlines, for example, separated its maintenance business from the main airline, and has an extensive training program for training young Saudis in aircraft maintenance. If we do not have qualified Saudis to maintain Saudia aircraft and insist on hiring poorly or unqualified Saudi technicians we would be jeopardizing passenger safety, and planes along with revenue will be dropping out of the sky.

Persistent citizen complaints have not been met with meaningful monitoring and supervision to implement standards of services rendered. A lot of money is wasted, and archaic rules and outdated systems make problems worse.

There is a need for good practices,such as those applied in more advanced countries, to create centers for Research and Innovation. These centers could provide research and analysis on key issues; promote creative solutions to improve quality of services; inspire ideas for decision makers to use in tackling tough issues; offer opportunities for the public to connect with officials; and a platform to share expertise. Such centers could enable officials to engage in dialogue with civil society. They could offer more transparency and collaborate with stakeholders in the community and consequently strengthen government services to the public. Perhaps it is time to replace traditional government departments with "Service Centers" that address citizen's needs as they arise. The staff of these centers would meet with citizens to determine priorities and eliminate problems.

The public should have access to more effective, well-designed and regularly updated websites and online forums to allow comments and questions online.

Decision makers are required to plan a broader strategic reorganization to address our shortcomings. Private-sector collaboration, civic engagement and participatory practices can be more effective in identifying obstacles and providing solutions. The government must work with the private sector and not against it. An alliance between government and the private sector can facilitate the planning process. A coalition of civic organizations can work towards implementing an inclusive problem-solving approach and develop results-driven strategies.

Saudi Research Centers Promote Development

The lack of research centers in our region makes it very difficult for decision makers to get accurate data that can help to formulate social, economic and scientific policies. Al-Aghar Group Think Tank is a notable exception that should be commended for continuing to engage stakeholders in workshops and seminars with experts to address our national problems and build strategies based on scientific research and theories to advance our nation.

Enhancing the role of the Saudi family in order to achieve the national objective of transforming the Kingdom into a knowledge-based society was the theme of the latest workshop conducted by Al-Aghar. It was sponsored by its strategic partner The King Abdulaziz and His Companions' Foundation for Giftedness and Creativity (*Mawhiba*), which strives to increase the scientific and innovative talent of Saudi youth and promotes the gifted, talented and creative community.

The objective of the workshop was to support an academic study that would enable Saudi families to overcome the challenges they are facing and change the negative mindset that has delayed progress and development within Saudi society.

A distinguished group of private- and public-sector leaders adopted a scientific methodology to identify a focus group for the study, which included less-educated families who lack interest in knowledge or development.

These experts were divided into four teams, each representing a segment of society. According to research conducted by Al-Aghar, Saudi society is divided into knowledge families, families with educated parents who do not promote knowledgeable children, a larger segment that includes less-educated families who lack interest in knowledge or development, and finally poor, uneducated families.

Each team was required to come up with viable solutions to support the creation of the knowledge family and to promote the segment of society they represented in the workshop. The team of experts which included Shoura Council members, officials of governmental and non-governmental organizations, academics and media personalities, engaged in constructive dialogue analyzing the challenges that prevent the Saudi family from coping with modern developments. They addressed the fundamentalist way of thinking, which rejects global trends and applies negative attitudes that discourage creativity and innovative thinking, and urged that awareness campaigns be launched to highlight the dire consequences of not correcting social ills and refusing to apply global standards in daily life.

The participation of the Minister of Education Prince Faisal Bin Abdullah in the workshop challenged the participants to introduce innovative solutions to reach the national objective of creating a more knowledgeable society.

The Secretary General of the King Abdul Aziz Center for National Dialogue, Faisal Al-Muammar, who was also among the participants, added valuable input about the existing tribal culture and the need to enhance the positive role of the religious establishment to influence the development of the knowledge-based family.

The team of experts outlined four major essential mechanisms to support their mission, namely to promote the roles of the mosque, academic institutions, the media and civil society. Friday sermons should carry interesting messages that emphasize the importance of seeking knowledge as an Islamic obligation of every citizen. Schools should offer programs that involve parents in their children's academic progress and encourage them to recognize the potential of their young ones.

A more active media role was recommended with awareness campaigns featuring well-known artists or sports personalities. Social messages can be very effective if they are delivered daily through radio, TV and social media to reinforce the spirit of innovation and academic excellence.

Another recommendation was the establishment of mentoring programs and the promotion of role models from within society. Prominent personalities could change the negligent attitude of parents and encourage them to make more meaningful attempts to provide love and quality time for their children. It was even suggested that a guidebook for the ideal parent should be prepared and distributed with birth certificates nationwide.

The discussions highlighted the need for the government to exert more effort to upgrade the educational system so as to produce more qualified graduates who are capable of mastering the technological and scientific advancements of our time. It was also suggested that incentives and rewards be given to those who implement a knowledge-based approach in their work.

The experts urged extended government and private sector support for strategic research and emphasized the need for more government funding for research centers in the fields of science and technology. There is also a need for alliances between government agencies, the religious establishment, academic institutions, NGOs and the media to initiate more effective programs that will expedite the knowledge-based process.

The experts finally concluded that less-educated families in society require immediate national attention to be transformed into knowledge families.

The *Mawhiba* and Al-Aghar alliance is indeed an ambitious attempt to build the appropriate environment and prepare the younger generation for making a contribution toward developing a knowledge society based on innovation and talent.

Addressing Social Ills

Admitting our social ills is a first and very encouraging step forward towards reforms.

Princesses are patronizing the nationwide awareness campaign to educate women about their rights, offering legal and social assistance to the victims and providing centers to care for the abused.

Princess Hissa Al-Shalaan, wife of Custodian of the Two Holy Mosques King Abdullah, supported the Human Rights Commission nationwide awareness campaign, and Princess Adela bint Abdullah is the active deputy chairperson of the National Family Safety Program. Princess Adela opened a seminar in Abha titled, "The Role of Judicial and Security Institutions in Fighting Family Violence." She also inaugurated the national family safety programs awareness campaign in Tabuk and Madinah in an effort to reach out across the nation to spread awareness and protect the Saudi family and accelerate reforms.

Researchers conclude that the lack of awareness about rights is the main problem facing our society. They stressed the problem lay in the individuals who violate religious teachings and follow aberrant customs and traditions. According to the national family safety program, one in every six women is verbally, physically or emotionally abused every day, and 90 percent of abusers are men, usually husbands or fathers.

151

We need to recognize that the reason the Saudi family is suffering is because a large segment of our society still insists on holding on to old customs and traditions, and they refuse to modernize or adopt a more progressive way of life. Male-dominated Saudi families often ignore the rights of women and deprive them of the privileges afforded to menfolk.

The lifestyle of strict segregation and the controlling attitude of dominating male family members are factors blocking the progress of our whole society. There are many families that impose a segregated lifestyle within the one family, not allowing brothers and sisters to meet the in-laws or enjoy a family outing or event together. Consequently the lack of communication and quality time among the members of a family has deprived Saudis of family bonding and happiness.

Banning driving for women and not providing proper public transportation is another kind of abuse. It is unfair to neglect women and children and keep them prisoners in their own homes waiting for a male to take them out for a breath of fresh air or a visit to the doctor or a meeting with family and friends. It is no longer acceptable for the man alone to enjoy a life of luxury while ignoring the needs of his family.

The Saudi family is threatened by the failure of the society to adapt to economic needs that make it imperative for young married women to work so that the family unit can afford a more comfortable lifestyle. A woman by law cannot work without the consent of her father or husband; he can prevent her from working and choose where she may or may not work. By law, a woman cannot travel without the consent of a male guardian; he can stop her from attending a conference or spending her vacation with family and friends.

In an unprecedented move the Ministry of Culture and Information conducted a workshop to upgrade the quality of programs geared to address the challenges that the average family faces.

Badria Hagras, director of the Bahrain Broadcasting Service, and Dr. Nora Al-Soyan, head of Social Services in the National Family Safety Program at King Abdul Aziz Medical City, were guest speakers. They outlined the challenges facing Saudi and Gulf families and emphasized the need for media to come up with innovative and more advanced strategies to provide better programming and offer constructive guidance and direction to disintegrating and troubled families in the region.

Nawal Bakhsh, head of the Family and Child Section of Radio Riyadh, said that Saudi media should to play a bigger role to address the challenges facing the Saudi family today. These included domestic violence, juvenile crime, tribal disputes, sex crime, divorce, child-custody disputes, child marriages and many other social ills. She stressed the need to address these issues and urged media professionals to spread awareness and to help stop the violence against women and children in Saudi society.

The disappearance of the extended family lifestyle where the grandparents uncles and aunts had a role in guiding and monitoring the behavior of the children in the family and the absence of friendship and communication between parents and their children, are also reasons why many children tend to have destructive attitudes and bad behavior

The negative sermons of the preachers in the mosques that encourage men to marry second wives in order to be a good Muslim have caused the breakup of many homes and have resulted in creating hatred between siblings and family rivalries. It has also deprived many families of a better standard of living because a father with a limited income has to provide for two families.

The Saudi family today is living in a state of frustration. Women, children and the young in particular are discontented mainly because they are the victims of rigid and unjust rules and regulations that need to be revised to recognize to their needs.

The government has failed Saudi families by enforcing laws and regulations that breed nothing but unhappiness. Discrimination against women continues to be a source of a lot of misery for many mothers, housewives and young women of this country.

The government imposes restrictions on fashion shows, music concerts and film festivals even in a segregated environment or in public events. Teenage boys until recently were banned from entering malls, and girls were banned from entering the stadiums to watch soccer matches.

Until recently physical education did not exist in public girls schools, and the lack of exercise among women has led to the high rate of obesity, diabetes, osteoporosis and depression. Saudi youth is bored, and they are loitering on the streets. There are not enough sports facilities or parks, and movie theatres are nonexistent.

These frustrations have been communicated to officials, and they are being discussed in newspaper and on television. There have been promises and reassurances to address the issues, but in the meantime there is growing frustration among the average citizen who does not subscribe to the fundamentalist point of view that supports these restrictions.

Hopefully the nationwide campaign to halt family violence will also promote a healthier family environment and develop a more prosperous modern-day society. Until the problems facing the Saudi families are solved they will continue to be a source of misery. Without the necessary laws and regulations that can protect their disintegration, Saudi family life is under increasing threat in a changing world.

Raising Public Awareness of Health Issues

Some 52 million people are forecast to die annually in the region by 2030, up from the current annual mortality total that exceeds 36 million, if non communicable diseases (NCDs) are not controlled effectively. The Minister of Health Dr. Abdullah Al-Rabeeah delivered this dire prediction at the International Conference on Lifestyle and Non-communicable Diseases in the Arab World and the Middle East that was held in Riyadh Oct. 10, 2012. The Kingdom has pledged to support regional and international initiatives to combat NCDs. We are now globally committed to upgrade our medical services and scientific research to meet the standards of international initiatives to curb the disturbing growing rates of this disease sector.

The minister called on all stakeholders to redouble their efforts to combat the growing prevalence of NCDs.It would be such a shame if these calls fall on deaf ears and serious action to promote healthy living is not given serious attention. Every government sector, plus civil society and the private sector will be put to the test to show strong, sustained professional leadership to set national targets for the prevention and control of non-communicable diseases. Our present record of medical services is very poor, and it is time to address our failings.

The Ministry of Health initiative to raise health awareness and promote healthy living is a major development that needs support and encouragement by all government sectors and health professionals across the country. Medical researchers, the media, social scientists and activists are urged to work together to raise public awareness of healthy lifestyle characteristics, mainly the benefits of not smoking, healthy weight, healthy diet and leisure time plus physical activity. It is very disturbing how healthy lifestyles are ignored and not recognized by our society today. Children often eat at fast-food restaurants that serve food with high levels of fat, sugar and sodium. Shisha and cigarette smoking is prevalent even among the very young, and physical inactivity and obesity are prevalent nationwide. We need to see immediate implementation of government initiatives to modify detrimental lifestyles to support the prevention and control of NCDs.

In the January/February 2012 issue of CA: A Cancer Journal for Clinicians, which is available free online, the American Cancer Society reissued its guide for nutrition and physical activity during and after Cancer treatment. These reports should serve as resources for health-care providers, patient advocates and other stakeholders to improve the health and wellbeing of this rapidly expanding and high-risk population.

The high level of physical inactivity among the majority of Saudis has had serious implications for health. There is a pressing need to address negative lifestyles that have been associated with the development of chronic diseases, specifically heart disease, cancer, stroke and diabetes. According to the most recent studies there is a high incidence (43.3–99.5 percent) of physical inactivity among Saudi children and adults alike.

The decision to allocate a large budget to promote sports and physical education in Saudi schoolsis an important development, and it could protect our children frommany NCDs. Hopefully all schools nationwide will soon include physical education in their curriculum, and they will be provided with adequate sports facilities to exercise and play sports. Medical research has proven that physical education and sports in schools is beneficial for both children and for the educational systems. They are necessary for the development of children's fundamental motor skills and physical competencies, which can influence their physical wellbeing later in life. They also can support the development of social skills and social behavior, self-esteem and pro-school attitudes, and, in certain circumstances, academic and cognitive development. Committed, trained teachers and coaches should manage physical education in our schools. Informed parents, who can significantly influence change and provide the desired healthy lifestyle for our children, should also support it. Inefficiency, red tape and bureaucracy should not sabotage the initiatives of the Ministry of Education.

Communication and information technology could also be utilized to spread better health awareness and nutritional education. The media can play a bigger role in changing the prevalent behavior and mindset that is detrimental to the wellbeing of all members in society. Activists, opinion leaders, bloggers and social media users can influence change and address the reckless and negative attitudes that are harmful to our future generation.

The international conference on lifestyle delivered major recommendations to promote the prevention and control of NCDs. The participants urged the need to share strategies, tools and cost-effective interventions with other countries in the region to improve health care for non-communicable diseases. They also called for building capacity and adopting a research agenda to provide essential access to treatment and care. This will require funding and assigning some of our best specialists who can contribute towards this global cause and national goal

The international community has positioned the non-communicable diseases as central to progress and economic growth. A more effective national policy to address social and economic detriments to health, and a more vigorous campaign to enhance the role of health education in contemporary society is the need of the hour.

Antiquated Laws and Regulations

The ongoing judicial reforms that recognize international laws are fundamental requirements for sustainable economic development in Saudi Arabia. Legal experts and the business community received very well the establishment of an independent Economic Tribunal in the Kingdom to deal only with investment and trade issues. They described the development both as a positive move that could improve the investors' faith in the Saudi business environment and as a major step towards the enhancement of foreign investment in the Kingdom.

At present there are numerous commercial and industrial disputes that have been going on for years. The present court system did not have the efficiency to resolve them. The experts welcomed the development during a special forum on the new "Saudi rules of arbitration and its impact on investment in Saudi Arabia." They outlined the significance of the new arbitration system that would allow parties to resort to international rules that may not be stipulated in the Saudi system. The new system will also address the lack of qualified Sharia experts by giving an opportunity for non-Sharia graduates to arbitrate.

The legal experts hailed the new system as needed to address the reluctance of foreign investors to invest in Saudi Arabia. They hoped that the new rules of arbitration would ensure greater transparency and provide a speedy settlement of all foreign and domestic disputes.

However, the business community has reiterated the need for the development of efficient government agencies to meet the needs of the new legal system. They stressed the importance of upgrading administrative departments in order to implement more effectively the measures stipulated by the new arbitration system.

Meanwhile, Saudi investors are also wary of other legal challenges facing the business community in the Kingdom. They are constantly calling for the elimination of rules and regulations detrimental to the success of their businesses and incompatible with the needs of today's business world.

The Saudi business community is waiting anxiously for the elimination of the legal guardianship rule imposed on women and the discriminatory practices in the workplace. The Chambers of Commerce continue to lobby for new laws that would protect the interests of working women. They include providing adequate transportation to work; adequate maternity leave; reasonable working hours; workplace nurseries; equal pay and medical insurance.

Businesses complain of the strict segregation laws that tend to delay work procedures and are the cause of inefficiencies and poor managerial standards. It also taxes the companies with extra facilities and unnecessary procedures that, if removed, could save them a lot of time and money. Several other steps would accelerate the delivering the potential that women could offer to the commercial life of the Kingdom. These include: enforcing laws based on the quota system, which could guarantee more job opportunities for women; enforcing stricter rules to address negative attitudes, which could stop the harassment of women in the workplace; and the implementation of policies that encourage the employment of qualified women in leadership and executive positions, which would boost the business environment and help us develop a more prosperous economy.

It is about time we replace the antiquated rules with progressive regulations that address our needs. The old school of centralized rules must be upgraded with new rules of management that delegate work to qualified personal who can get the work done without delay. It is time we eliminated the restrictions imposed in the workplace in order to appease the extremists in our midst. Legislators are required to act with a greater sense of commitment to serve public interests.

Unfortunately the influence of hardliners still exists, and they exercise their control over the business community and society as a whole. Businesses suffer and are delayed or abandoned because of legal restrictions. Foremost among these legal hindrances are permit regulations. The business community is burdened by the delay in issuing permits that are required from more than one Ministry or government department before any investor can finally initiate any business plan.

Permits can and do take months to process due to bureaucracy and the outmoded application requirements. Local investors are hoping for new legal procedures and an ease on the restrictions imposed by overly rigid rules and regulations. Legal restrictions and tedious regulations stand in the way of business opportunities.

Policy makers are called upon by the business community to encourage and show more support for the struggling small- and medium-size businesses (SMEs), which generate a large proportion of the country's wealth and act as the nurseries for future large-scale businesses. Legal changes need to be put in place to improve the enforcement of contracts to help smaller enterprises obtain loans and ease the risks to make lending less restrictive.

Social activists continue to reject rules and regulations that violate the legitimate rights and civil liberties of Saudi citizens. The hardliners who continue to exercise legal control over our economic liberty are a threat to the nation's economic prosperity.

Legal experts and the business community are encouraged by the establishment of the new system of arbitration and are hopeful that it will be followed by more financial, legal, and labor reforms.

Codified Sharia laws to serve justice

The injustice of denying divorce to many women who are suffering under the hands of cruel, vindictive husbands was the subject of discussion on the MBC channel last week. Popular talk show host, Daoud Alshiryan hosted Dr.Suhaila Zain Alabideen of the National Society for Human Rights, a prominent judge, a lawyer, and a divorced woman who was the victim of a greedy father and an elderly man. She was married at 14 and suffered her husband's cruelty, miserliness and foul behavior for years because a judge refused to grant her the divorce until she paid the dowry spent by her father.

Alabideen emphasized that judges need to understand the concept of *Khul3*or redemption that was applied in the case of this victim of a cruel husband. According to Sharia law, redemption or *Khul3* is only applied in cases of divorce, whereby the wife agrees to pay an amount of money to a non-abusive husband to buy out her freedom. She explained that abused women who are living in miserable conditions have the right to ask for a divorce. Judges need to be reminded not to apply *Khul3* unjustifiably. It is time to put an end to the distorted application of *Khul3* that allows the husband to take advantage of his wife's vulnerability and demand compensation in return for her release.

The popular program succeeded in addressing divorce cases due to cruelty, neglect, failure to provide, psychological abuse and violent behavior causing injuries and mental distress. The panelists discussed cases where women have to suffer the humiliation to report to a police station and produce medical evidence and gather witnesses to testify in courts. They also brought to light other cases when women were deprived of seeing their children. The husbands would threaten to harm the children or would be cruel to them to take their revenge on the mothers seeking divorce.

The Sharia scholar reiterated that enforcing misinterpreted Sharia rulings is the reason behind the injustice towards women and children in our courts today. Judges should not remain indifferent to the long-term suffering of women at the hands of husbands who refuse to grant them divorce and are cruel to their children. Women have a right to ask for divorce and have the freedom to remarry and to hope for happiness and a life of dignity.

The scholar brilliantly disputed discriminatory rulings against women in the name of Islam. Her eloquence and scholarly knowledge of Sharia gave her the authority to debate the controversial issues concerning the legal rights of women in Islam. She used examples from the Quran and *Sunnah,* and she identified misinterpretations or weak *Hadiths* that are not strongly authenticated and are often applied in divorce cases denying women justice and fair trial.

Alabideen is not alone in criticizing the discrimination against women and the cruelty of many men in Muslim countries. Young women today have become intolerant to the injustice in our courts. They are on Twitter and on Face Book criticizing the negligence in addressing grievance and injustices. Educated women today continue to demand for their God-given rights, and they will not be satisfied until justice is served. The only way to ensure women's confidence is by implementing legislation to enforce a fair and legal action that reflects the true teachings of Islam.

Alabideen said during her hot discussion that there is a need to address the ambiguities in the rulings of our *Ulamas*, and we need to influence a more humane attitude towards women. She said social injustice against women requires effective, codified Sharia law so that both men and women would be aware of women's legal rights, and violators would be held accountable for mistreatment and abuse. Discrimination against women will come to an end only when there is a written code of Sharia law

The well-respected advocate of women's rights in Saudi Arabia has often pointed out the mistakes about religious discourse in many talk shows and television interviews. However, she holds that there has been positive progress on human rights taking place in Saudi Arabia. "We are moving on the right path as a result of the acceptance and understanding of human rights, where every member of the family has a right to a good life based on Islamic values," Alabideen said.

Chapter 10

THE MODERNIZATION PROCESS

The Modernization Process

Reformers have now taken a more active role in combating theracism and extremism that have crept into Saudi society. Media and social activists are working hard to reverse this negative image that is alien to Muslim nature. The moderates are striving to regain their pride and respect in Islam. There are many voices in society calling for the need both to separate tribal heritage from religious precepts and to reject the former and embrace the latter in order to lead the faith to a position reconcilable with modernity and a world containing many different values and beliefs.

The modernization process has begun, and there are many efforts towards reform. King Abdullah University for Science and Technology, (KAUST) the first co-ed university in the Kingdom, is the King's vision for a beacon of research and knowledge to address the challenges of global significance to serve the Kingdom, the region and the world.

Princess Nora University, the world's largest university for girls, offers many majors to open new opportunities for women in the workforce, while Effat and Dar Alhekma Universities are among the best academic institutions for girls in Jeddah. Their talented graduates are among the most highly qualified in the Kingdom. They represent a new breed of young women who can influence change and contribute to modernizing the Kingdom.

The new universities established across the Kingdom will provide higher educational opportunities for all citizens. The new faculty for Islamic economics and finance that was established at Makkah's Umm al-QuraUniversity will have four departments: economics, financing, banking and capital markets, and insurance. The specialized graduates of Islamic economics will be able to serve Islamic banking, which has gained global recognition, and their expertise will be very much in demand.

King Abdullah's scholarship program includes more than 100,000 students currently studying abroad. The program allows Saudi students to go to the world's best universities for bachelor's, master's and doctoral degrees. Scholarship students are provided with monthly stipends, tuition, as well as travel expenses and a cash allowance for books. Students are rewarded with bonuses for excellence in academic performance.

The government has also initiated various educational and vocational training programs to build professional and vocational skills among Saudi citizens.

162

In-line with global opportunities the government has finally taken a stand against the hard-line policies of religious scholars who were against any efforts towards changing the weekend days.

THE royal decree on the weekly holidays is an important and practical decision that is in the interest of the nation and its economy. The business community has been calling for this move to change the weekend holidays from Thursday and Friday to Friday and Saturday for a long time. Saudi businessmen breathed a sigh of relief and asserted that the move will have a positive impact on the business environment and would help Saudi Arabia develop a more prosperous economy.

Technically the kingdom had only three common working days with the world , and four days of disconnect from global business opportunities. Productivity was poor and businesses suffered within the Gulf countries because there were only four working days of the week. There were no clear cut timings and there was a lot of wasted opportunities for quality productivity. The banking sector could not fully utilize its potential either. Business leaders believe the move would help them in creating global partnerships to foster our business and trade connections with the rest of the world.

One of the challenges that we face in Saudi Arabia today is to adapt and compete with the global business community and address our present-day needs. The conventional policy of constraint stands in the way of implementing flexible programs to ensure progressive opportunities for the business and work environment. It permits the influence of negative and un-progressive attitudes to exist depriving many businessmen of better prospects for trade and business ventures.

In Diversity there should be unity

Government campaigns to counter radicalization aredelivering an 80-90percentsuccess rate according to government officials. The Internet-based counter radicalization campaign, "has enabled Islamic scholars to interact online with people looking for direction or religious advice." It has succeeded in steering away many of our young people from extremist recruiting sources and has been instrumental in eliminating the threat of terrorism in the country.

In 2009 the decision to expand the Senior Council of *Ulamas* to include 21 members from all schools of Muslim thought, was aimed at combating extremism and serving Saudi society as a whole. Today the inclusion of *Ulamas* mastering the four main schools of thought, namely the *Hanbali,Shafei, Maliki,* and *Hanafi* give the council ample options in the interest of all Muslims based on the Quran and the *Sunnah*. This development initially renewed the trust towards government initiatives to combat extremism and implement reforms. However, the austere Wahabi doctrine derived from the *Hanbali*School is still dominant.

Saudi women and the younger generation do not wish to comply with the strict lifestyle of the *Salafis*, a doctrine which enforces the complete segregation between sexes, the *niqab*(veil)and a rigid lifestyle proclaiming modernity as un-Islamic. Many expected to hear more from the moderate *Ulemas* in the Supreme council who adhere to different schools in order to usher in a more moderate Muslim lifestyle that supports a more flexible attitude towards the public and is in tune with the realities of the 21st century.

Unfortunately the influence of hardliners still exists, and they continue to exercise their control on society. Women are still waiting for the elimination of the guardianship rule and others are still hoping to be relieved of the rigid *Hai'a* (religious police) control that infringes upon social liberties.

In 2010 after many *fatwas* issued by some extremist *Ulamas* caused a lot of public uproar and international criticism and as a result, the king banned all *fatwas* that were not authorized by the Supreme Council of *Ulamas*. Websites and call-in shows on religious channels that aired illegal *fatwas* were also shut down. Extremist scholars were fired from their posts. However, ultra- conservatives still see themselves as above all this and are hostile towards anyone who does not conform to their views They use social media to express their condemnations and their rigid interpretations of Islamic Shariah law.

In an effort to promote tolerance and moderation, and encourage national solidarity the National Dialogue Center conducted 2,677 training programs run by certified trainers. However, the center was not as effective as either hoped or intended. Hardliners were the dominant participants, and they defended their extremist views dismissing modernity and change.

In 2012 Dr.Abdul-LatifAlsheikh,chairman of the board of Senior *Ulama,* was appointed as the head of the *Hai'a* because he is considered to be a more moderate scholar. He reduced the *Hai'a's* undercover patrols and stopped his staffers from chasing minor offenders. He lifted the ban on young men entering malls and admitted it was a mistake. He also ordered his staffers not to speak harshly to women who wear makeup to the malls, but to advise them gently about decent behavior or else speak to their guardians. The new head publicly announced these instructions to 500 *Hai'a* field staffers during an official publicized guidance program. Will they abide by the rules and refrain from their public harassments? That remains to be seen.

The arts and cultural events that are appreciated by talented Saudi artists are still rejected by the extremists. They continue to condemn traditional folk music and dance at the annual Janadriya festival celebrated by many intellectuals and artists from all over the Kingdom.

Another annual celebration that is held annually is the historic Souk Okaz event. Every year a variety of cultural activities are presented that include seminars, poetry competitions and folklore dances

The Janadriya festival in Riyadh and the Souk Okaz festival in Taif are among the most famousof the festivals sponsored by the government and widely celebrated every year with cultural activities and folk music, an antiques exhibition, folk dances, handmade Bedouin products, plays, live theater productions and poetry recitations and competitions. International and Arab world personalities, prominent intellectuals and artists from abroad and across the Kingdom are invited each year to celebrate their historic status.

Janadriya Festival started as a camel race; today it represents a crossroads where poetry, intellect, culture, art, theatre, as well as heritage and history meet.

Souk Okaz was an ancient destination for Arab intellectuals and poets and people passionate about culture and literature. It has been revived in the tourist resort of Taif to promote culture and creativity in our country.The annual gatheringis an opportunity for Arab poets, thinkers and men of letters to exchange views and ideas. At Souk Okaz, prizes have been introduced to honor outstanding poets, craftsmen, folk artists, photographers, calligraphers, painters and sculptors. Prizesinclude cash awards amounting SR 1.1 million, for the best poet and best folklore artist.The Souk Okaz Prize for the best handicraft ranges from SR 150,000 to SR 350,000. The objective is to encourage more Saudi nationals to work in the handicrafts sector.

The organization of art and theatre festivals aims to develop the level of performing arts and sponsors talented young people to provide them an opportunity to develop and display their talent. However, they are all government-chartered associations and face many restrictions in order to appease the ever-present extremists.

The Government continues to sponsor book fairs and literary clubs ,which are very popular among academics and the literary circle. However, it does so against the wishes of the extremist element, which deliberately creates incidents during these events to show its discontent.

Social activists expect the process of modernizing Saudi Arabia will continue to face further delays without the elimination of the hard-line elements are working hard to preserve the status quo. These obstructionists continue to use distorted principles of Islam to subjugate women, restrict civil liberties and suppress progressive thought. In order to expose the reality of the extremists'ideology Senior *Ulemas* need to use the four schools of thought effectively as a base for their rulings instead of only one.

Government reformers need to remove the cultural barriers and take a more active role in combating extremism, tribal racism and sectarian conflicts, which continue to threaten the Saudi social fabric.

There are still influential clerics who are blocking the changes that could modernize the existing system, and they control and infringe on people's privacy rights. One example is Sheikh Albarak, a 77 year-old scholar from Alqassim - who said that those who support the mixing of sexes in Saudi Arabia should be executed, and he attacked satellite channels that aired entertainment and music shows.

The half-hearted attempts to rein in the hardline *Ulamas* who see themselves as arbiters of correctness and thought are slowing the pace of progress. The attitude of extremists is always hostile towards anyone who does not conform to their views. These ultra conservatives are the ones who are depriving citizens of their basic rights to choose a modern lifestyle that does not go against the moderate schools of Muslim thought. They are standing in the way of social and political reforms.

The support and tolerance of the austere Wahabi clerics could create dangerous sectarian or religious conflicts threatening the harmony and stability of this society. The government continues to challenge the powerful clerics of the Najd region. *Wahabis* are followers of Muhammad ibn Abdul-Wahab, the 8th century theologian from Najd who advocated a stricter

Hanbali Muslim school of thought. They often denounce those who differ to them in juristic matters. Wahabism is a movement that gained dominance in Najd through an alliance between Muhammad ibnAbd al-Wahaband the House of Saud.

The *Hai'a* (religious police) is another block in the way of modernizing Saudi Arabia.

The once-revered Commission for the Promotion of Virtue and the Prevention of Vice has become a hated organization and a source of misery to the women and the youngwho represent the largest segments of society. The media has reported many stories of the *Hai'a's* abusive behavior that violates the basic human rights of citizens in malls, on the streets and in many public places. After thousands of public complaints of violent and sometimes criminal behavior of *Hai'a* towards innocent, law-abiding citizens the government ordered official investigations into the conduct of *Hai'a* staffers.

The government employs *Hai'a*"advisers" to enforce Sharia law and provides them with vehicles to monitor public behavior and impose the black abaya as the only permissible dress for all women. The *Hai'a*often harasses women if they wear makeup in malls or if they wear a colored abaya; forces people to pray; enforces a strict segregation law; harassesand arrests any man or woman who is in the company of anyone who is not a legal guardian, usually in the form of husband, father uncle or son.

There are 3,500 official members of the *Hai'a* and thousands of "volunteers."They are accompanied by police officers for protection. Upon their instructions the officers on many occasions forcefully carry out an arrest. The victims are usually kept for 24 hours at the *Hai'a* headquarters and have to sign a statement to refrain from repeating the so-called offense. The whole idea is to spread fear and force people to comply with their rigid rules and restrictions

They enjoy a large budget from the state to carry out their much-resented activities. There are many voices in society calling for their disbandment. The Saudi government has been embarrassed over several incidents of the *Mutawas'* (another popular name for the religious police)confrontations with diplomats and their abusive behavior towards foreigners, Muslims and non-Muslims alike, yet the government is still hesitant to dismantle the organization and refuses to reserve the power to arrest for moral misconduct or misdemeanor only to the police force.

In diversity there should be unity.

Fighting fanaticism and extremism is a national duty. Saudi religious scholars, academics and media officials are keen to promote national solidarity and social unity within the Kingdom.

The King Abdulaziz Center for National Dialogue in its fifth annual dialogue to promote national solidarity continues to pursue national and inter-religious dialogue, in order to address the influence of rejectionist voices and create a consensus to foster national unity and promote the acceptance of diversity within Saudi society.

During the past decade the Center has pursued its objective to encourage more tolerance for religious diversity and to rein in the forces of religious extremism in the Kingdom. It has brought together leading religious figures from different sects, and hard-line scholars who have persistently refused to accept the other.

King Abdullah has called for all schools of Islamic thought to be officially included in national dialogue. It is hoped that the engagement of different religious sects in dialogue will end divisions and establish a commitment to coexistence between all Saudi citizens as the basis for national unity.

The real challenge for participants in the national dialogue is to promote political and social stability and achieve national unity through acknowledging and accepting differences, rather than denying or suppressing them.

There have been encouraging initiatives lately between the different sects in the Kingdom. The interaction and constructive dialogue between prominent religious leaders, such as Sheikh Hasan Al-Saffar and Sheikh Salman Al-Oudah, is a welcome development toward national unity and social stability. The religious leaders called for mutual respect and dignity and rejected incitement, violence and ignorance.

There is no denying that sensitivities still remain with respect to sectarian differences, and that other sects are not entirely accepted by a considerable segment of society; however, the King Abdulaziz Center for National Dialogue has been instrumental in making great progress toward creating wider acceptance and tolerance for diversity of opinion.

The government has recognized that the religious environment can become very dangerous when unqualified people issue extremist *fatwas*. Under the current official policy, the issuing of *fatwas* has been limited to the Senior Council of *Ulema*, which represents the consensus of officially recognized senior scholars. The impression of consensus is intended to promote a sense of national unity.

In the past there was little effort made to recognize diversity within the Kingdom, but today religious scholars engage in discussions of Islamic discourse rooted in moderation and justice both within the Kingdom of Saudi Arabia as well as outside it. The participants in constructive dialogue continue to call for a culture of tolerance and respect for alternate interpretations of Islam.

They reject ultraconservative interpretations that influence ongoing divisions between sects within Islam that are not in keeping with their own interpretation, and they refuse to divide the world into Muslim and non-Muslim. However, some extremist religious scholars in all sects and all faiths remain resistant to interfaith dialogue and insist on maintaining boundaries between different Muslim sects and between Muslims and non-Muslims.

There are still many challenges confronting senior religious scholars who have strongly supported dialogue and have called for the elimination of disunity, extremism, and ignorance. They have publicly opposed the deviant ideology of terrorism and violence in the name of religion.

In November 2007, King Abdullah paid a historic visit to the Vatican in order to address misconceptions about Islam and to promote interfaith dialogue. A number of other meetings between religious scholars and intellectuals were held to promote the concept of dialogue and greater religious understanding, beginning in Makkah, then in Madrid, the United Nations, Geneva and finally culminating in the establishment of the King Abdullah Bin Abdulaziz International Center for Interreligious and Intercultural Dialogue (KAICIID) in Vienna.

King Abdullah has often warned of sectarianism, tribal differences and favoring one segment of society over the other as elements that threaten the unity of the country.

The secretary-general of the King Abdulaziz Center for National Dialogue, Faisal Al-Muammar, said that forums have succeeded in establishing a common ground for healthy dialogue between different segments of the Saudi community. He also stressed that "division in its various forms destroys unity and conciliation that builds brotherhood under the umbrella of one nation," adding that "national unity is the lifeguard of the nation when ideologies and people's interests are mixed.

"The National Dialogue has a vision regarding renewing religious speech so that it is in line with modern times, without changing the basics," he said. "It is essential that religious speech be renewed according to the changing times and changes from one generation to another. In the past, religious speech had its own style, and in our current age it needs another style, which is in line with development and people's needs that suit their culture, understanding, and social and psychological status while maintaining the basics of Sharia Law."

CONCLUSION

The reforms continue despite the confrontation between tradition and modernity. Hard-liners still continue to exercise powerful influence over policymaking and social norms. It will need another generation to usher in an age of enlightenment that will allow the Kingdom to lead the Muslim Nation to global prosperity.

However, the determination to pursue the reform path that King Abdullah initiated has inspired the whole nation. In the course of eight years much has been achieved. Unfortunately the greatest challenge still remains to be the defeat of the extremist ideology that has hijacked this Holy Land and has jeopardized the future of many innocent youths.

The reform movement is geared towards keeping the society competitive in a very competitive world, and strives to muzzle the obstructionists and replace pointless, deviant misguidance with wonderful opportunities for the young men and women in this country.

The clock is ticking; however, and time certainly is not limitless. Population continues to grow, requiring more jobs, more housing and more economic activity in general while domestic demand for energy grows and threatens to diminish the nation's oil exports to fuel more autos, power more homes and provide more drinking water. The nation has to move forward as it has grown too much, too fast to even consider standing still. Stagnation at this point will lower our standard of living as we watch other nations progress and snatch up the economic growth and potential that could have assured our next generation the kind of lifestyle and prosperity to which we have been accustomed

The strong public support for King Abdullah's reforms by the moderates, and the concerted efforts to initiate cultural, social and academic activities all will help Saudi Arabia modernize. The success of the movement will create a better world for the younger generation — the sooner, the better.

22405942R00103

Printed in Great Britain
by Amazon